Notes

Introductory and concluding sections do not include citations, as each piece of information is cited within the body of the text. Unless otherwise mentioned, all references to Islam refer specifically to schools of Islam within the Sunni sect.

Acknowledgments:

I would like to thank everyone who has provided me intellectual and emotional support throughout this project, including my family, friends, Ariella, and Walter Russell Mead.

Table of Contents

Introduction
Three Empires Meet in a Graveyard
    1. Rollercoaster of Love
    2. Ghosts in a Graveyard
    3. Kristmas in Kabul
A Hundred Years Added to my Life
    4. The Shah Goes to Rome, Never Comes Back
    5. Exodus
    6. A Gift Handed on a Golden Platter
Conclusion
Works Cited

Introduction

The Soviet-Afghan War served as a critical turning point in Asia's geopolitical map. At the superpower level, the war marked the culmination of a strategic shift in the trilateral relationship between the United States, the Soviet Union, and the People's Republic of China. On an ideological level, the war marked the first of many stages of a militant Sunni Islamic revival that seeks to overturn colonial borders and replace them with a transnational Islamic movement. Both the Sino-Soviet Split and the rising force of political Jihadism brought the Soviets into Afghanistan, and both forces played a major role throughout the conflict.

The Soviets did not invade Afghanistan to protect the recently installed communist government. The invasion of Afghanistan primarily served as a last ditch effort to secure their southern flank against a Sino-American anti-Soviet bloc. The relationship between the Soviet Union and the People's Republic of China (PRC) had turned sour as early as 1954, just five years after the establishment of the PRC and nine years after the end of the Second World War, as leaders from both sides quickly found that despite the common ideological narrative that both sides were trying to cast, they remained in a state of constant competition against each other. By the time that the Soviets invaded Afghanistan, the two countries had already spent the last twenty years supporting insurgent groups and states against each other. In 1979, when the Soviets invaded Afghanistan, they were responding to a changing geopolitical landscape marked by the recent Chinese invasion of Vietnam, the Sino-Indian War, and border skirmishes between the Chinese and the Soviets. As Soviet troops flooded Afghanistan, The PRC instantly began to play a major role in supporting the resistance to the Soviets, a fact that was quickly picked up on by Soviet intelligence. Perhaps Asia is merely too crowded for two major land powers, as it is clear that Chinese and Soviet maneuvers against the other brought the two into the war in Afghanistan.

With little exception, all of the aid money that the United States, the PRC, and their allies in Saudi Arabia, the United Kingdom, and Egypt gave to the mujihadeen after 1979 was routed through Pakistan's Inter-Services Intelligence (ISI). The ISI though, did not begin their relationship with the Afghan mujihadeen in 1979, but had instead been aiding anti-Kabul rebels since at least 1973 as part of a long-running strategy toward Afghanistan. For Pakistan, Afghanistan has represented a landscape to paint over with increasingly radical forms of Islam.

The United States and its allies in the conflict, as they sent money through the Pakistanis, were not working to promote a national liberation conflict. They were instead working *against* a national liberation movement that had been in the midst of a long running struggle against the Pakistani State for thirty years. Pakistani support for anti-Kabul rebels, the support that would ultimately spark the war, was fundamentally based on a strategy of 'Islam over Tribe.'

There is no such thing as either a Pakistani or an Afghan people. There is not now, nor has there ever been, a strong enough national identity to encapsulate the people of either country. Historically, Afghanistan has been ruled by guns and gold, while Pakistan emerged from the British Raj and the subsequent partition as a nation that existed primarily as a Muslim counterpart to India. Few in the region base their identity on being Afghans or Pakistanis, and the issue of how to either divide or define the millions of people of different tribal or ethnic identities as citizens of their states is a problem that will continue to plague both countries for the considerable future. The lack of cohesive political identities in the Afghanistan-Pakistan region has been and will continue to be a fundamental and unanswered question for Pakistan, which needs to subdue Pashtun, Baloch, Sindh, and other ethnic quests just to hold itself together. In order to quiet the constant threat of ethnic separatism, Pakistani strategy has been to promote increasingly radical versions of political Islam when confronted with ethnic nationalism, a strategy which had repeatedly failed—until the Soviets invaded.

In the decades between the death of Joseph Stalin in 1953 and the Saur Revolution in 1978, Soviet strategy in Afghanistan had involved supporting the Durrani Dynasty and the subsequent regime led by Mohammad Daoud Khan to buffer the USSR's southern border. These regimes served as protection against the American-backed government in Pakistan to the South, the Chinese to the east, and other Baghdad-Pact containment structures to the Soviets' southwest. Supporting the Durrani Monarchy, which included a number of Pashtun nationalists such as Daoud, had effectively meant that the Soviet Union was supporting the concept of redrawing state borders in South Asia around ethnic lines, a process that would have dissolved Pakistan altogether. The prospect of a Soviet-backed national liberation movement in the Pashtun tribal lands forced the Pakistanis to support mosques, madrassahs, and militant groups which promote radical and violent forms of Islam.

Throughout the 1960s and 1970s, the Soviet Union opened its universities to Afghan students who were subjugated to rigorous political and ideological indoctrination. As these Afghan communists gained more and more power in Kabul, they became more and more radical, essentially using each other as echo chambers from which they could develop increasingly radical ideas. As the communists in Kabul radicalized, so did the Islamists, and by the late 1960s, the two opposing ideological movements were violently clashing in the streets of Kabul. The Pakistanis, who saw communism as a vehicle with which the Soviets and their Afghan allies would promote a Pashtun national movement, increasingly supported and built infrastructure for the propagation of radical forms of Islam such as the Quranic literalism of the Deobandi and Wahhabi schools.

The Soviet invasion and the subsequent influx of weapons, money, and non-lethal aid from the United States, the People's Republic of China, and Saudi Arabia appeared to quiet this struggle, as the Pakistani ISI ensured that nearly all of the money went to the Pashtun Islamic fundamentalist leaders that Pakistan hoped would hold the country together. The theory stood that if Pakistan supported Pashtun Islamist leaders, the Afghans, who were majority Pashtun, would unify for the defense of Islam rather than squabbling over ethnic and tribal conflicts.

This strategy though, proved insufficient, as national and ethnic conflicts that started while the Soviets were still occupying Afghanistan continued well after they left. In the years following the Soviet pullout, the Pakistanis managed to consolidate Pashtun political life under the banner of the radical Deobanidi Jihadis known as the Taliban, but the Tajiks and Uzbeks continued to rally around local leaders such as Ahmed Shah Massoud and Abdul Rashid Dostum. These schisms led to a civil war fought primarily along ethnic lines that continued until the arrival of American forces in the final months of 2001.

The Soviet-Afghan War, a war which involved the importation of many ideologically motivated foreign fighters, did provide support to the notion that radical Islam could, at least temporarily, serve as a unifying force. Despite their levels of internal conflict, the imported fighters, most of whom were Arab, did manage to unite around a clearly defined enemy and to cooperate well enough to continue the movement outside of Afghanistan. Whether or not such unity can continue though, remains a challenge that political jihadists around the world will continue to struggle with as they deal with the chaos that is currently embroiling the Middle East and North Africa.

Upon close inspection, the Soviet-Afghan War exists as a struggle on two fronts. On one level, the war was a struggle between the Chinese and the Soviets as both jockeyed for power and influence in Asia. On the other level, the war was a struggle between the divisiveness of tribal identities and Pakistani attempts to impose political unity under Islam.

__Three Empires Meet in a Graveyard__

The crowded landmass of Asia offers little room for strategic error. The rivers, deserts, mountains, and colonial lines that carve up the map into national borders leave states surrounded by competitors, enemies, and potential conquerors. One wrong move by any Asian land power opens the door to the possibility of encirclement by hostile neighbors, each of which has a strong historical case for mistrust in those around them. In the mid-1950s, two large states, the Soviet Union and the People's Republic of China (PRC), grappled with the reality of being major powers on this crowded land-mass, briefly held together by an ideological identity, the Soviets and the Communist Chinese quickly began to drift away from each other as both competed for influence both in Asia and around the world. The subsequent maneuvering that both sides took against each other, marked by two wars, border skirmishes, and the diplomatic opening between the PRC and the United States, culminated with the Soviet invasion of Afghanistan in 1979 and the military aid that the Chinese rushed to deliver to the anti-Soviet mujihadeen.

The insurgency that overtook Afghanistan in the mid-1970s had little to nothing to do with the People's Republic of China or the United States, other than the indirect support that both sides gave to rebels through military aid to Pakistan. The Soviet Union though, out of fear for security on its southern border, was pushed into the war by the geopolitical maneuverings and strategic cooperation between the Americans and the Chinese. The workers of the world failed to unite and the communist regimes of the PRC and the USSR maneuvered against each other in Vietnam, pursued opposing strategies toward India, and fought border skirmishes that killed dozens of soldiers from both sides. As both sides rushed to gain friends, arm insurgents, and defend their allies, both the Soviet Union and the Chinese were driven to act by a perceived strategic encirclement by the other. At the superpower level, the Soviet-Afghan War emerged from a clash between the national security ambitions of the Soviets and the Chinese.

1. Rollercoaster of Love

The drunken revelers flooded Times Square, waiting for the ball to drop. As 1979 approached, the countdown began, and at the stroke of midnight the confetti flew and the cheers began. Similar celebrations had already been taking place for hours as citizens around the world erupted in the jubilation that typically ushers in a new year. Most of these revelers had no idea that the year that they were bringing in would be the most tumultuous year for global politics since the end of the Second World War. By the end of the year, China had invaded Vietnam, the Shah of Iran was deposed in an Islamic revolution, Deng Xiaoping was beginning his famed transformation of China, and the Soviet Union celebrated Christmas by flooding Afghanistan with Soviet paratroopers. 1979 was the year that twenty years of super power politics culminated in a fundamental shift in the trilateral relationship between the United States, the Soviet Union, and the People's Republic of China.

One of the year's most important events in great power politics occurred before the revelers were even be woken up by their screaming hangovers. Following a joint communiqué that had been agreed to in mid-December, the United States formally recognized the People's Republic of China as the legal government of China while maintaining the position that Taiwan was to be part of a united China.[1] This meant that for the first time, the United States was switching its diplomatic recognition from Taiwan's Republic of China (ROC) to the mainland's People's Republic. This communiqué and the overall thaw in relations were the culmination of years of effort on the parts of both the United States and the PRC.

Following the consolidation of control over mainland China by Communist forces in

---

[1] Joint Communiqué on the Establishment of Diplomatic Relations between the People's Republic of China and the United States of America.

1949 and the subsequent Guomindang retreat to Taiwan, the United States was left wondering where its diplomatic relations should stand. In the early 1950s, the United States had considered going down what seemed like the obvious route and simply recognizing the two Chinas as separate political entities, but both the People's Republic of China (PRC) and the Republic of China (ROC) strongly rejected any attempts at joint recognition, leaving American diplomatic recognition standing with Taiwan's ROC.[2] By August of 1954, the crisis between the two Chinas was becoming increasingly difficult to manage. The PRC was shelling the islands of Quemoy and Matsu, two disputed islands occupied by ROC forces but geographically closer to the PRC. With the Korean War battles between the United States and the PRC still fresh in American minds, it was obviously who President Eisenhower would choose to support. The United States deployed three carrier battle groups to the strait, and drew up preparations for the use of nuclear weapons to resolve the crisis while rushing through a defense treaty with Taiwan.[3]

The First Taiwan Strait crisis left the United States and China in a state of uneasy hostility, but the greater effect was on China's relations with the Soviet Union. Sino-Soviet relations had always been uneasy, but following the end of the Chinese Civil War there was hope that the two socialist giants could reconcile their differences and form a joint front against the western world. On September 8, 1954, Khrushchev took a side, throwing his weight behind the People's Republic of China and essentially extending the reach of the Soviet nuclear umbrella to cover the Strait of Taiwan.[4] To an outsider, this would look like the type of

---

[2] Kissinger, Henry 134-135
[3] Ibid 134-139
[4] Dikotter, Frank 79-80

ordeal that would strengthen the relationship between the USSR and China, but Khrushchev was outraged. From Khrushchev's perspective, the Chinese had manipulated him into entering a dangerous crisis over a conflict that had no strategic meaning for the Soviet Union. The Soviets, who saw themselves as the centerpiece of a global socialist revolution, were increasingly beginning to understand that the Chinese would not be the reliable socialist allies that they wanted. This view was affirmed in 1955 when Mao Zedong refused to join the Warsaw Pact, and instead helped to form the non-aligned movement in protest over Soviet regional hegemony.[5] Relations with the USSR would never recover.

Relations between the PRC and the USSR continued to decline over the next two decades, as both countries began to view the other as more of a competitor than as a potential friend. In a short territorial war between China and India over territory, the Soviets lashed out strongly against the PRC, even going as far to accuse Mao of having strategically aided the United States during the Cuban Missile Crisis.[6] A trade war erupted between the PRC and USSR, as the Chinese sought to undercut the price of Soviet exports and lure third world nations away from the Soviets with low prices and attractive aid packages.[7] As the American war in Vietnam began to rage in the mid to late 1960s, the Chinese and the Soviet Union found themselves at odds over who was pulling the strings in North Vietnam. While in reality, the Vietnamese were their own actors who were willing to exploit both the PRC and the USSR for military aid, the Chinese and the Soviets were both deeply worried about the possibility of Vietnam falling into the other's orbit.

---

[5] Kissinger, Henry 143-146
[6] Ibid 168
[7] Dikotter, Frank 104-106

In a 1965 conversation with Ho Chi Minh, Zhou Enlai articulated that "The Soviet revisionists want North Vietnam to talk with the US, to put the NLF [National Liberation Front] aside and sell out its brothers."[8] In a later conversation with Pham Van Dong, the North Vietnamese Prime Minister, Zhou accused Soviet aid of being "insincere" and said that the Vietnamese would be "better off without it."[9] These remarks were emblematic of China's attempts to lure the Vietnamese into the Chinese camp, but the attempt was in vain. To the Vietnamese, who had been crafting an anti-Chinese national identity over centuries of deep engagement with China, a few years of aid and a shared political ideology were not enough to change their deep-seeded views. Relations between China and North Vietnam deteriorated, and by 1978, the Chinese leadership considered Vietnam to be firmly within the Soviet sphere.[10]

In March of 1969, just a few weeks after the inauguration of American President Richard Nixon, China's Cold War with the Soviet Union began to turn hot. Deadly clashes along the Ussuri River nearly led to war between the two socialist giants. Over a million Soviet troops were moved to the Chinese border. Skirmishes broke out along the borders of Xinjiang province, resulting in the destruction of at least one Chinese battalion.[11] The chances of a large-scale war increased with each day of border confrontations and hot skirmishes. The border dispute would eventually cool down, but not before catching the eye of President Nixon. The conventional American view was that China was, while not firmly in the Soviet camp, still an ally of the Soviet Union that sought to undermine American goals in Asia wherever it could. Chinese actions in Korea, Vietnam, Taiwan, and India, among others, only

---

[8] Arne Westad, Odd, Chen Jian, Stein Tønnesson, Nguyen Vu Tungand, and James G. Hershberg 29
[9] Ibid 85
[10] Kissinger, Henry 287-293
[11] Ibid 187-188

supported this increasingly out of touch view. President Nixon though, was less likely than many of his peers and predecessors to see the world through the Cold War ideological lens, and was more interested in realist geopolitical strategy. He saw China as less of a socialist adversary, and more of a potential American hedge against the Soviet Union. His view that the United States should support the Chinese against the Soviet Union may have had strategic merit, but it was certainly controversial at home. Regardless, the realist president pushed ahead with his attempts to open relations with China.[12]

With a million Soviet troops arranged across its northern and border, a hostile India to the Southwest, a Soviet-aligned and increasingly hostile North Vietnam to the Southeast and hundreds of thousands of American troops still fighting in South Vietnam, the Chinese felt the noose of a strategic encirclement taking shape. Facing a potential hot war from all sides, the Chinese began to see the advantages of opening relations with the United States. In a 1970 conversation with American journalist Edgar Snow, Mao Zedong was reported to have said that:

> "If the Soviet Union wouldn't do [point the way] then he would place his hopes on the American people... In the meantime, the foreign ministry was studying the matter of admitting Americans from the left, middle and right to visit China... [Nixon] would be welcomed because, at present the problems between China and the U.S.A. would have to be solved with Nixon. [I] would be happy to talk with him, either as a tourist or as President... China should learn from the United States[13]"

Henry Kissinger would later claim that this interview (which unfortunately would not be published for another six months) was nothing more than an attempt to communicate with

---

[12] Ibid 185-190
[13] Snow, Edgar

the Nixon Administration. Kissinger believes that Mao thought that the transcript would end up in the hands of the US government. Unfortunately for all sides, Edgar Snow had long been ostracized from the American government community for his perceived pro-communist agenda, and the interview failed to make waves in Washington.[14]

What began as a slow and low level series of openings accelerated into higher level talks as it became clearer that both sides were serious about engagement. A series of low level talks in Warsaw transitioned into American attempts to open communication channels with PRC diplomats in France, Romania and Pakistan. China attempted to communicate through embassies in Norway and Afghanistan before taking the openings in Romania and Pakistan.[15]

On December 8, 1970, The Pakistani Ambassador to the United States brought a handwritten letter from Zhou Enlai to Kissinger's office. The letter proposed, under the auspices of negotiations over the American presence in Taiwan, for a top level American envoy to visit Beijing. Zhou stressed that both Mao and Lin Bao had approved this communication.[16] The White House accepted the invitation to Beijing, but would not allow the talks to focus solely on Taiwan. The Chinese would need to be willing to discuss "the broad range of issues which lie between the People's Republic of China and the U.S."[17] In January, Kissinger received another message from Zhou, this time describing Taiwan as the only issue to reconciliation (notably excluding the ongoing Vietnam War) and personally inviting President Nixon to China. The White House accepted the offer of sending an emissary but chose not to acknowledge the invitation to the President.[18] In April of 1971, Mao replied with

---

[14] Kissinger, Henry 195
[15] Ibid 187-195
[16] Ibid 197-198
[17] Ibid 199

an unusual diplomatic overture—the invitation of the American ping pong team to Beijing. The now infamous round of "ping pong diplomacy" opened the door to further negotiations. A more conventional reply from Beijing invited a high level American to Beijing, naming Secretary of State Rogers, National Security Advisory Kissinger, or President Nixon himself as possible emissaries. By May, the Americans had agreed to send Nixon and Kissinger to meet Mao.[19]

The extraordinary journey that led to the Nixon/Kissinger summits to China is widely and accurately credited with opening up a new era of Sino-American relations. Without Kissinger's secret 1971 summit and Nixon's public summit in 1972, it is doubtful that the two sides could have found it within themselves, in either the midst or in the aftermath of the Vietnam War, to warm relations with their public enemies. Fear though, brought the Chinese to the table, and opportunity brought the Americans. While Soviet-American relations were quite cold during this time period, the United States did not face the type of ongoing crossfire with the Soviet Union that Mao was facing. China was facing the existential threat of strategic encirclement and hot war, and retreated from the concept that China was fighting a great ideological war against the United States. Mao Zedong, usually seen as a man of ideology and principle, dropped his pretenses and put himself at great risk to open up a dialogue with the United States.

The communiqué released at the end of these summits was carefully crafted to ensure the warming of relations without seriously hitting upon touchy subjects. Both sides expressed opposition to hegemony in Asia (a thinly veiled statement of joint interest against the Soviet

---

[18] Ibid 199
[19] Ibid 199-202

Union), while the United States acknowledged that there was only one China, announced the eventual withdrawal of American forces from Taiwan, and pushed for a peaceful resolution from both sides of the strait.[20] While essentially a way of saying that the United States had not significantly changed its view on Taiwan, the wording was sufficient to please both sides and to ease the blockage that the Taiwan issue had long been in Sino-American relations.[21]

---

[20] Joint Communiqué of the People's Republic of China and the United States of America
[21] Kissinger, Henry 231-233

2. Ghosts in a Graveyard

It had been less than twenty years since the United States and the Soviet Union nearly went to war over the Quemoy and Matsu Islands. Few observers in 1954 could have possibly imagined that the United States would pick up Beijing as an informal ally against the Soviet Union in such a short period of time. It took skillful diplomacy, a recognition of rare opportunities, and the failure of the Soviet Union to reconcile with China, but the impossible had been done. It remained unclear though, how this new quasi-alliance would play out. Mao Zedong's death in 1976 prevented him from living to see the establishment of formal relations with the United States, and the power vacuum that resulted from his death left relations in a state of uncertainty until 1979, when Deng Xiaoping, a reform minded and western oriented leader, emerged to take the reins. Deng, a longtime ally of Mao who had been purged during both the Cultural Revolution and during the succession crisis, was looking to take China in a new direction. While for the most part Deng continued the foreign policy of Mao, he differed greatly on how he viewed the Soviet Union. Where Mao had seen an abstract threat, Deng saw a clear and present danger.[22] A more pragmatic man than Mao, Deng dropped whatever apprehensions still existed about working with the United States in favor of a policy of cooperation against the Soviet Union. Nowhere would this be more apparent than on China's western flank, in the mountainous tribal lands of Afghanistan.

The Soviets would invade on Christmas. Troops would pour into Afghanistan, killing the President and declaring a new government. This invasion and leadership change though, was merely the end result of a series of leadership changes and geopolitical challenges facing

---

[22] Ibid 292-293

Afghanistan and the rest of Asia in 1979. It was not the first time that decade that the Soviet Union had helped to overthrown an Afghan government, nor was it the year's first major war in Asia.

King Zahir Shah was merely the continuation of a Pashtun dynasty that had ruled Afghanistan since the fall of a Persian dynasty in 1747. When Zahir Shah took the reins in 1933, few could have foreseen that he would become the last Shah of Afghanistan.[23] In 1973 though, Zahir Shah was overthrown by his cousin, Mohammed Daoud. Daoud, an ally of the Parcham faction of Afghanistan's communist party, was Zahir Shah's former Prime Minister, and was known to be friendly to the Soviet Union, although there is insufficient evidence to directly tie his coup to the Soviets. While he may have acted alone to seize power, the rise of a Parcham leader in Afghanistan certainly would have looked to Moscow like the culmination of decades of Soviet strategy in Afghanistan.

The Soviet Union, through the KGB, had spent the last two decades working to promote communism in the poor and remote country. Nearly 4,000 Afghan military officers had gone north to the USSR for military training and indoctrination.[24] By the late 1970s, ideological power in Kabul had become a struggle between the moderate Parcham communists and the radical Khalqi communists. The Soviet Union, unaware that the communists in Kabul were vastly outnumbered by the Islamists in the rest of the country, thought that their strategy would work as well in Afghanistan as it had in Uzbekistan and Kazakhstan, where ideological training had helped to bolster Soviet control. The tribal and bloody nature of Afghan politics though, quickly began to undermine Soviet strategy.

---

[23] Coll, Steve 303-304
[24] Coll, Steve 61

After using the Parchams for his coup, Daoud quickly began to purge them from his government in an attempt to steer away from the Soviet Union. He wanted to play the US and the USSR against each other for aid money, and by 1978, Daoud was becoming a target of both his Parcham faction and of the more extreme Khalqis, who were led by Mohammad Taraki and were increasingly fed up with his purges and his lack of support for communist policies.[25] In April of 1978, sensing that his grip on power was weakening and facing growing civil unrest, Daoud initiated a series of mass arrests of both Parchams and Khalqis. By this point though, it was too late. On April 28, 1978, Daoud was killed in a Soviet-backed coup. Hundreds of Soviet military and political advisers, including members of the KGB, swarmed in to help Taraki build a police state and promote communism.[26] Taraki declared the foundation of the "Democratic Republic of Afghanistan," and signed a "Treaty of Friendship, Cooperation, and Good Neighborliness" with Moscow.[27] Taraki quickly unveiled an agenda that aimed to include relatively radical and rapid reforms to Afghanistan. Many tribal Afghans, sensing that these reforms were being imposed from abroad, were quick to begin resisting.

To a westerner, many of Taraki's reforms seemed perfectly reasonable. Taraki sought to promote literacy for both boys and girls, banned dowries for brides, and attempted to give women a choice in who they married.[28] He wanted to modernize Afghanistan away from what was essentially a feudal system while increasing the rights of women in one of the world's worst places for women's rights. He used Soviet aid to build schools, hospitals, telephone

---

[25] Kaplan, Robert D 176-177
[26] Coll, Steve. 61-63
[27] Wawro, Geoffrey 374
[28] Coll, Steve 62

lines, and infrastructure.[29] In a country already filled with Islamic radicalism, tribalism, and anti-western sentiment, these reforms did not go well. They were also not helped by the fact that Taraki was a brutal authoritarian leader who sought to do away with any opposition while building a cult of personality around himself. With the help of his Soviet advisers, Taraki was building secret police networks, loyal communist militia units, and jailed over 12,000 people—most of whom were religious and social leaders—who stood in his way.[30] Perhaps his most offensive act though, was the replacement of Afghanistan's Islamic green flag with a communist red flag.[31]

To understand the resistance that would captivate the whole of Afghanistan over the next ten years, one must turn west to Iran, and southeast to Pakistan. A wave of political Shia Islamic radicalism had overtaken Iran in the last half of 1978, leading to the overthrow of the American-backed Shah in early 1979. Fed up with the relatively secular and authoritarian governments that had been backed by the United States and the Soviet Union across the Muslim world, the Islamic revolution in Iran was as much a revolution against Cold War geopolitics as it was against the Shah. Ayatollah Khomeini sought to use Iran as a launching point to provide the entire Islamic world with the ideology—namely Shia Islam—that he hoped would overthrow the Cold War western-backed order and implement a new series of Islamic republics under his sphere of influence.[32]

To Afghanistan's southeast stands Pakistan, a state with a strong Islamic identity that was being run by General Muhammad Zia-ul-Haq. Zia, who had overthrown the elected

---

[29] Wawro, Geoffrey 374-376
[30] Coll, Steve 61
[31] Wawro, Geoffrey 375
[32] Wawro, Geoffrey 361-362

government of Zulkifar Ali Bhutto in 1977,[33] was a fairly moderate Islamist, but due to the conditions that Pakistan had emerged from following the partition of India in 1947, Pakistan's entire national identity was based around Islam. With fears of Balochi and Pashtun separatism, Zia knew that Pakistan needed an aura of Islamic spiritualism to hold the country together.[34] While he certainly feared these separatist forces quite a bit, Zia had far more to fear from India. With the backing of the Soviet Union, India had defeated Pakistan in three wars, one as recently as 1971, and constant skirmishes continued to cement the two countries' positions as mortal enemies. As the Soviet Union begun to exert more and more influence throughout Afghanistan in 1978 and early 1979, it was clear to Zia that he risked being encircled by India to the east and an Indian-aligned USSR to the west. It was time for Pakistan to fight for its own survival.[35][36]

    The Pakistanis were not the only ones worried that they were being encircled. By 1979, the Chinese fears of the Soviet Union had only been exacerbated by a deteriorating situation in Southeast Asia. Following a Vietnamese invasion of Cambodia in 1978, the Chinese feared that the Soviet Union would use Vietnam to achieve hegemony in Southeast Asia, while simultaneously pushing into Afghanistan and then further into Pakistan, nearly completing the encirclement of China. In November of 1978, Vietnam followed Afghanistan's lead in signing a Treaty of Friendship and Cooperation with the Soviet Union and joined the Soviet Comecon trade block.[37] The Chinese did not see the Carter administration as doing anything

---

[33] Kaplan, Robert D 33-34
[34] Ibid 109
[35] Wawro, Geoffrey 375-383
[36] Crile, George 103-104
[37] Kissinger, Henry 291

to protect China, which like Pakistan, was fighting a struggle for survival.[38] China and the United States had agreed to normalize relations in 1978, but the United States was simply not providing the help that China needed to play its part in an anti-Soviet bloc.

In a January, 1979 interview with Walter Cronkite, Jim Leher, and Frank Reynolds, Deng Xiaoping remarked that "we must deal in a down-to-earth way with Soviet hegemonism... we do hope that the United States will adopt more effective measures, more strong measures to deal with the challenges posed by hegemonism." When asked to clarify remarks that the United States was in the midst of a strategic defeat, Deng replied that "for quite some time now, the Soviet Union is on the offensive, whereas the United States is on the defensive... because of these changes in position, the main hotbed of war is now the Soviet Union."[39]

In February of 1979, Deng Xiaoping became more explicit in his calls for American aid, claiming that "If we want to be able to place curbs on the polar bear, the only realistic thing for us is to unite. If we only depend on the strength of the U.S., it is not enough. If we only depend on the strength of Europe, it is not enough. We are an insignificant, poor country, but if we unite, well, it will then carry weight."[40] Deng was being very deliberate and clear with his words. The United States had allowed the Soviet Union to dictate the rules of the game, whether it was in Southeast Asia or in Afghanistan. Facing the loss of the Shah in Iran, the loss of the Vietnam War, and public backlash against the CIA, the United States had fallen behind. China was willing to bring the fight back to the Soviets, but it needed help.

---

[38] Ibid 294-295
[39] "Interview of Vice-Premier Deng Xiaoping by U.S. TV Commentators."
[40] Kissinger, Henry 299

The American help didn't come for the Chinese in Southeast Asia, and on February 17 of 1979, Chinese troops poured over the border into Vietnam, winning a short but brutal war. The Chinese quickly withdrew their forces but the message was clear—Deng was willing to use significant force to prevent a Soviet encirclement. China had managed to do enough damage to Vietnamese forces to prevent their further expansion in Southeast Asia, while also showing the United States that they were players in the game to contain the Soviet Union. The United States responded by sending Vice President Mondale to China in August of 1979 to discuss postwar strategy, and Secretary of Defense Brown visited China a few months later to discuss anti-Soviet aid to Thailand and a post Pol Pot Cambodia. The United States also began to sell non-lethal military equipment, such as helicopters and military vehicles to China, and dropped its resistance to NATO allies selling lethal military equipment to China.[41] In 1979, fear of the Soviet Union had once again provoked China into acting, and once again the end result was to bring the United States and China closer together against the Soviets. It was in Afghanistan, on China's western border, where this new strategic partnership would have its greatest effect.

While a new era of US-China relations was bringing in the new year, the resistance in Afghanistan was escalating. With Taraki seeking to extend his grip on power, Afghans were beginning to organize an armed resistance against his rule and against his Soviet advisers. The Iranian revolution exported a wave of militant political Islam into Afghanistan, concentrating in the Western city of Herat, the disproportionately Shia city which lies near Afghanistan's border with Iran. The Herat garrison of Afghanistan's army rose up against

---

[41] Ibid 209-313

their Soviet advisers in March of 1979, killing over a dozen Soviet advisers.[42] The Soviets responded by aiding the Afghan army in a bombing campaign that killed over 24,000 Afghans and nearly leveled Herat. Mutinies and desertions in the Afghan Army spiked, leading to a loss of over half of its strength in the first months of the resistance.[43]

As the resistance in Afghanistan begun, the world took notice of the potential trouble that the Soviets were causing. A US embassy cable from June of 1978 claimed that "The new government of the Democratic Republic of Afghanistan (DRA) is overwhelmingly dependent on the Soviet Union. It cannot stay in power without help. It relies one hundred percent on the Soviet Union for military assistance." The cable went on to say that "the new leaders of the DRA… clearly fear the possibility against them from both internal and external actors." The cable also said that it was not apparent that there were any foreign actors organizing the resistance.[44] This cable clearly hinted at an opening, and as early as March of 1979, as Herat was burning, the CIA sought to enter through this opening.

On March 28, the CIA's National Intelligence Officer for the Soviet Union wrote that there was a real possibility that the Taraki regime would begin to disintegrate, the Soviets would provide extensive assistance to save it, and foreign actors, including potentially Pakistan, Iran, and China, would provide aid to the resistance. This scenario would force American involvement to protect Pakistan from the Soviet Union. He went on to ask the extent to which the United States would be willing to aid the Afghan resistance.[45] As the resistance picked up in the early half of 1979, it was already clear that the potential for an

---

[42] Coll, Steve 62
[43] Wawro, Geoffrey 377
[44] "Six Weeks after Afghanistan's Revolution"
[45] Gates, Robert M 134-136

international crisis was increasing with each day.

The internal dialogues among Chinese leaders are far less open to the public than those of the United States are, but the Chinese political class was certainly paying close attention to the brewing situation on their western border. Facing the prospect of strategic encirclement, China called upon the world to seize the opening in Afghanistan. Just two days after the CIA began to investigate the possibility for action, the Chinese weekly paper *Beijing Review* sought to spell out the situation:

> "With Cuba and Vietnam as its falcon and hound, the Soviet Union has started a southward offensive from Africa, the Middle East to Southeast Asia to seek strategic war materials, occupy strategic military bases, and control oil transportation lines. It is trying as best it can to compete its global deployment to attain world supremacy. The hawkish Soviet challenge poses the peace-loving countries and people all over the world with a pressing question: How is the Soviet Union's hegemonic aggression and expansion to be met? Make comprises and concessions, or unite and struggle against it?"[46]

This opinion piece, in what was likely a reflection of the views of the Chinese Communist Party, would go on to advise the world to form a broad united front against hegemonism, because "only by doing this can we check [the Soviet Union's] rampancy, ease the tense situation, and put off the outbreak of a world war and safeguard the peace and security of the world."[47]

The 1950 Treaty of Friendship between China and the Soviet Union was due to expire in 1980, and by April of 1979 the Chinese had informed the Soviet Union that the treaty would not be extended. Just four short months after diplomatic relations with the United States had

---

[46] "How to Deal with Soviet Hegemonism."
[47] Ibid

been formalized, China was formally cutting its treaties with the Soviet Union. In just two short decades, China's alignment in the Cold War had flipped.

By June of 1979, *Beijing Review* made the Chinese view on Afghanistan even clearer. The Taraki regime was essentially declared to be a puppet of the Soviet Union. Moscow wanted to pacify Afghanistan to further its strategic goals.[48] Afghanistan was simply a staging ground for a larger scale southward drive, which included fomenting unrest in Turkey, Pakistan, and Iran, particularly with Pakistan and Iran's Balochis, who live in the Balochi regions in Southwestern Pakistan and Southeastern Iran.[49]

This gets to the heart of how the Chinese political and foreign policy establishment viewed the globe in early 1979. The United States was seen as being in retreat around the world, and the Soviet Union was pushing towards global hegemony. The first stage of achieving this was taking the fight away from Western Europe, where the Americans and their NATO allies maintained most of their strength, but instead pushing into parts of the world that the United States was in retreat from. Following the American defeat in the Vietnam War, the Soviet Union was free to use Vietnam as a springboard from which it could launch into Southeast Asia, putting Cambodia, Laos, and eventually Thailand under the control of Vietnam and into the Soviet orbit. At the same time, the Soviet Union could exploit the American loss in Central Asia that had come with the Iranian Revolution, and could use the chill in US-Pakistani relations that Zia's coup and Pakistan's nuclear drive had inflicted upon the Carter White House. After stabilizing the situation in Afghanistan, The Soviets would be able to use the unrest that they were perceived to be encouraging in Iranian and Pakistani

---

[48] Xin, Chanlin
[49] Xin, Ping.

Balochistan as an excuse to capture, at the very least, the Pakistani port of Gwadar that juts out from Balochistan. Russia has historically desired a warm water port in the Indian Ocean, and now the Chinese feared that the Soviet Union saw an opportunity to seize one for its navy in Thailand and Pakistan. With a Soviet navy able to access the South Pacific through Vietnam and the Indian Ocean through Thailand and Gwadar, the Soviet Union would be able to control or exert considerable influence over the Strait of Malacca, the Strait of Hormuz, and the Suez Canal. With control or influence over these vital choke points, the Soviet Union would have achieved control over the world's oil supply and therefore the world economy. It was absolutely vital that the Soviet Union's southern drive not be allowed to extend beyond Afghanistan.[50]

While there were some in the United States who saw the same possibilities that the Chinese saw, most Americans in the CIA and other American foreign policy circles did not think that the Soviet Union would commit itself to an invasion of Afghanistan, even as the rebellion against Taraki and his Soviet advisers was picking up steam. National Security Adviser Brzezinski, thinking that the Soviets were just fighting the Afghan mujihadeen, wanted to help to ensure that the resistance was able to continue. In early July of 1979, he recommended to President Carter that the CIA provide non-lethal aid to the Afghan resistance. On July 3, President Carter accepted Brzezinski's proposal, and the CIA was allocated half a million dollars to spend on non-lethal assistance for the Afghans. This amount was just a drop in the enormous bucket of aid that the United States would provide over the next ten years.[51] As American aid began to trickle in, the situation continued to deteriorate for

---

[50] "Moscow's 'Dumb Bell' Strategy"
[51] Coll, Steve 66-67

Taraki and the Soviet Union. With twenty-four of Afghanistan's twenty-eight provinces in full scale revolt,[52] the Soviets weighed their options. On March 17, as the situation in Herat was breaking down, a special session of the Politburo sought to deal with the situation in Afghanistan. Recognizing that resistance was fomenting and that Taraki's rule was imperiled, Russia began to put blame on the United States, China, Pakistan, and Iran for fomenting resistance. With thousands of insurgents fomenting unrest in the countryside, the Army division that the Soviets already had inside of Afghanistan was not enough to stop what the Kremlin essentially viewed as a foreign invasion of Herat. The Kremlin was also growing increasingly concerned that Taraki and Amin—Taraki's Minister of Foreign Affairs and right-hand man—were growing out of touch with the scale of the insurgency. They decided to increase levels of military and humanitarian aid in an attempt to support Taraki. The most important lines of this meeting though, are the demonstration of how important Afghanistan was to the Soviets. Over and over again, it is stressed that under no circumstances could Afghanistan be lost. The survival of the Taraki regime was of the utmost importance to the Soviet Union, and the Soviets, fearing the prospect of encirclement by the PRC and United States, would do whatever it took to maintain their grip on their southern neighbor.[53]

The Politburo's claims that the US, Iran, Pakistan, and China were all aiding the rebellion as early as March 1979 are quite extraordinary, and hopefully the potential declassification of secret documents will provide substance to these claims. Pakistan had been aiding the mujihadeen since at least 1973, and Iran was certainly providing ideological support to the rebels in Herat, but the United States did not authorize any aid until July of

---

[52] Wawro, Geoffrey 374
[53] Meeting of the Politburo of the Central Committee of the Communist Party of the Soviet Union, March 17, 1979

1979, and the Chinese were unlikely to have started providing direct support until February of 1980.[54] Regardless though, this view from the Kremlin helps to explain their coming moves. From Moscow it appeared that an uneasy situation was being made worse by subversive action coming from the United States, China, Pakistan, and Iran. The Soviet Union would need to work with Taraki to prevent further deterioration.

The Islamic resistance in Afghanistan was only getting worse for Taraki. Revolts like the one in Herat had spread to Jalalabad, where officers mutinied against their Soviet advisers, murdering them in the process. The Soviet Union drafted a letter to Taraki, urging him to stop fighting with his rivals within the government, to soften his stance toward the Islamists, and to work with the mullahs to find a way to convince the general public that communism and Islam were compatible. Taraki ignored the advice and sought to confront the rebels head on. Following the mutiny in Jalalabad, Taraki's forces massacred hundreds of men and boys in Kunar. Taraki consistently asked for more Soviet troops, while the Soviets consistently replied that they would provide aid, but that Soviet troops would only worsen the situation against the Islamists. Ultimately though, it wasn't the Islamists who did away with Taraki. Over the past year, infighting and power struggles had consumed the relationship between Taraki and Foreign Minister Hafizullah Amin, and in a true Afghan fashion, Amin would betray and overthrow Taraki. On September 14, 1979, Taraki was smothered with a pillow, and Amin was declared President of Afghanistan.[55]

As the first trickles of American money and aid were being funneled into Afghanistan through Pakistan's Inter-Services Intelligence agency (ISI), Amin's coup convinced the

---

[54] Eftimiades, Nicholas. 100-102
[55] Coll, Steve 65-69

Americans that more was possible. The fact that Amin had overthrown a leader who the Soviet Union had publicly championed just weeks before convinced the Americans that the Soviet Union had lost control of the situation. The National Security Council took up the position that the coup had been done in defiance of the Soviet Union, and that it was no longer possible to see how the Soviets would maintain a grip on the country using just Afghan forces. Through the coup, "The Soviets have just been pushed a big step nearer to their moment of truth in Afghanistan. In this game of 'ten little Afghans,' there is now only one left."[56]

The National Security Council was correct to assume that Amin had acted without backing from the Soviet Union. The KGB, witnessing Amin's gradual rise to power over the last few months, had actually been planting false stories about his cooperation with the CIA in the Afghan media to discredit him in the eyes of the Afghan Communist Party. After the coup, in a bizarre twist of fate, the Soviets began to believe their own propaganda.[57] Suspicious that Amin was a CIA agent, the Soviet Union became increasingly convinced that Amin was working to shift Afghanistan from a pro-Soviet into a pro-American state. By October, the KGB was recommending that if Amin was to turn in an anti-Soviet direction, which they believed to be in the cards, it was prudent that the Soviet Union "introduce supplemental proposals about measures from our side."[58] With a division of Soviet troops already inside the country and with more massing on the border, it wasn't hard to see what these "supplemental proposals" might consist of.

The Americans were unaware of the extent to which the Soviets distrusted Amin.

---

[56] What Are the Soviets Doing in Afghanistan?
[57] Coll, Steve. 68-70
[58] Memorandum on Afghanistan

Aware that he was in fact, not a CIA agent, the Americans likely assumed that the Soviet Union was aware of this fact as well. The CIA still maintained the belief that Amin would see the enormous threats to his regime from the increasingly large-scale Islamic insurgency, and would be forced to ask the Soviets for additional military aid, as Taraki had done. The Soviets would be most likely to respond by increasing shipments of arms and advanced weapons platforms, including helicopters and tanks. The Soviets might even have been willing to provide pilots and drivers for the weapons platforms, and may have even been willing to go as far as to send an airborne division to protect the regime in Kabul. The Soviets though, would surely have had to have recognized that due to the Afghan terrain and nature of the insurgency, securing the country outside of Kabul would have required a large-scale invasion. This invasion would require removing troops from the Chinese border to use in Afghanistan, which the CIA did not see as a good use of manpower. As the moment of truth arrived, the Americans were oblivious to how the Soviets were thinking about Afghanistan.[59]

The Americans did not share the Chinese view that the Soviets were using Afghanistan to push for global hegemony. While Cold War mindsets made just about every American in a position of power suspicious of Soviet intentions, the United States and the Soviet Union were still in a period of détente. While the two sides certainly did not trust the other, the Helsinki accords and the SALT II treaty, combined with the nature of the Carter Administration, gave Washington a less inherently nefarious view of the Soviet Union than the view from Beijing. In 1979, while the Americans were certainly uncertain over what exactly it was that the Soviet Union wanted in Afghanistan, the best guess seemed to be that the Soviets were eager to prop

---

[59] Soviet Options in Afghanistan

up a pro-Soviet state right on their weak southern underbelly, and were willing to support the success of communist revolutions around the globe for ideological reasons. Afghanistan was worth some military aid and a few thousand civilian and military advisers, but surely it would not be worth the enormous financial and military expenses that a full scale invasion would require.[60]

As the moment of truth neared, the Soviets, like the Chinese, saw themselves as being increasingly strategically encircled. Following the opening of diplomatic relations between the United States and China, the Soviet Union now had to contend with the possibility of China's enormous military population working to further pro-American and anti-Soviet strategic aims. The Chinese invasion of Vietnam had proven that China was now willing to use force on a large scale to counter the Soviets and their allies. The revolution in Iran and the subsequent seizure of the American hostages had brought a buildup of American troops in the Indian Ocean, and the new regime in Iran was opposed to the Soviet Union almost as much as it was opposed to the United States. The Americans and NATO had enormous force on the USSR's western flank, and were now preparing to station Pershing missiles in Western Europe.[61] The Soviets likely underestimated the extent to which relations had been damaged between the United States and Pakistan, and were increasingly becoming convinced (correctly) that the two countries were working together to undermine the Soviet goals in Afghanistan. The incorrect assumption that those two were also working with Iran and China to undermine the Soviet Union only served as confirmation bias for the idea that the Soviet Union was being encircled. Only Afghanistan remained as a pro-Soviet buffer between the USSR and its

---

[60] Ibid
[61] Tomsen, Peter. 161-163

enemies, and now the Soviet Union believed that their man in Afghanistan had been replaced by a CIA agent. The KGB begun to fear the potential for the deployment of Pershing missiles in Afghanistan, a direct threat to the Soviet's southern underbelly—the part of the country most poorly equipped to detect and protect itself from missile and aerial attacks.[62] The United States could then use the uranium deposits in Afghanistan to support Iranian and Pakistani drives toward nuclear weapons, further threatening the Soviet Union.[63] The idea that the United States would be willing to support Iran's Ayatollahs in the pursuit of a nuclear weapon may seem nonsensical, but it was a real possibility to the Kremlin in 1979. The situation in Afghanistan simply needed to be changed.

The Soviets plotted their next moves. The KGB under Yuri Andropov begun to work with a group of exiled Afghan communists led by Babrak Karmal and Asadullah Sarwari. Andropov recommended bringing additional troops into Afghanistan and positioning more troops on the border, for the exiled communists would be unlikely to be able to overthrow Amin without Soviet help. The KGB recommended a near immediate implementation of this conspiratorial operation to overthrow Amin. The Soviets needed to act to "allow us to decide the question of defending the gains of the April revolution, establish Leninist principals in the party and state leadership of Afghanistan, and secure our positions in this country."[64] The coup was imminent.

By early December, Brezhnev had agreed with Andropov that it was time for Amin to go. The military was to prepare to bring in 75,000 troops to stabilize the country.[65] As Soviet

---

[62] Coll, Steve 70
[63] Account of the Decision of the CC CPSU Decision to Send Troops to Afghanistan
[64] Personal Memorandum from Yuri Andropov to Leonid Brezhnev
[65] Account of the Decision of the CC CPSU Decision to Send Troops to Afghanistan

troops began to prepare for Amin's ouster, the KGB sought to lure him into a false sense of security. A wave of congratulatory messages and visitations from the Soviet Union, combined with a renewed thrust of civilian and military aid convinced Amin, who was unaware that the Soviets perceived him to be an asset of the CIA, that the Soviets had decided to back him. Amin requested direct Soviet military aid to help to protect him from the insurgents. The Soviets, who hadn't given this aid to Taraki, saw an opening and chose to exploit it. The Soviets sent a battalion of troops to "aid" Amin's security detail, and at his request, sent two full divisions to "protect" Amin's interests in Afghanistan's north. On December 7, these divisions provided cover for the exiled Afghan communist Babrak Karmal to be flown into Bagram airbase,[66] and by mid-December, KGB commandos were attached to the battalion that was charged with "protecting" Amin.[67] These KGB commandos would twice attempt to assassinate Amin, first with poisoned food, and then with a sniper rifle, but in both cases Amin's paranoia kept him alive.[68] It was becoming increasingly obvious to the Soviets what would need to be done. Amin must go, and it would require more than just covert action to do it. The Soviet Union would rely on its military to topple Amin and install Karmal.

---

[66] Coll, Steve 71
[67] Tomsen, Peter 163-165
[68] Coll, Steve 71

3. Kristmas in Kabul

As the Carter family prepared for a White House Christmas celebration, Soviet troops poured into Afghanistan. Plane after plane of Soviet paratroopers arrived at airports in Bagram and Kabul, while a motorized division secured land crossing points for further Soviet forces to enter Afghanistan through. By the end of the day, over 7,000 occupying troops were in Kabul, just a small fraction of what was to come over the next few days. Amin, who still mistakenly believed himself to be a Soviet ally, thought that these were the troops that he had asked for to help to clear the insurgency. It likely wasn't until the evening of the 27th, when his Soviet security detail turned on him and begun the assault on his palace, that he would realize what was going on. After a series of heavy battles, Amin was dead, and Kabul had completely fallen to the Soviets. On December 28, Radio Kabul announced that Karmal was the new President, Prime Minister, and Communist Party General Secretary of Afghanistan. In his first address to the nation, Karmal called for military and political aid from the Soviet Union, and the Soviets immediately followed his scripted calls for aid with more troops.[69] As the New Years revelers prepared to usher in the end of an extremely hectic year, Soviet troops continued to flow into Afghanistan. The brutal war that would kill over a million and displace another five million had just begun.

On December 26, the National Security Council and the CIA began to outline their strategy for the coming ten years. The Americans felt that the worst case scenario for them was for the Soviet troops to be able to quickly and effectively end the insurgency and pacify the countryside. The Americans believed that the Soviets were fully capable of taking on a

---

[69] Tomsen, Peter 163-178

lightly armed, poorly trained, constantly infighting, and badly coordinated bunch of uneducated and uncivilized rebels. While it would be impossible to beat them, the Americans felt that they could "make the operation as costly as possible to the Soviets."[70]

Zbigniew Brzezinski took a look at the regional balance of power and realized that over the past year, it had become horribly unbalanced. Iran, once a firm US ally and a vital part of the American containment strategy, had fallen into turmoil, and its new leadership was extremely hostile to the United States. Pakistan, a state the constantly seemed to be teetering on the brink of collapse, now faced a Soviet ally on its eastern front in India and a hostile Soviet army to the northwest. In a letter to President Carter on the 26th, Brzezinski wrote that Pakistan "is likely to be intimidated, and it could eventually acquiesce to some form of external Soviet domination." He also correctly claimed that following China's intervention in Vietnam, the Chinese would continue to see the Carter administration as unwilling and unable to restrain and contain the Soviet Union, putting their new-found alignment in jeopardy.[71]

In the past, Britain had used Afghanistan as a buffer to prevent the Russians from achieving their age old dream of a warm water port on the Indian Ocean. Now, with the region in chaos and the Soviets establishing a foothold in Afghanistan, Moscow had a chance to follow through on the strategic design that the Chinese (and now Brzezinski) believed to be its goal—to thrust southward into Pakistan or even Iran to obtain the port of their dreams. If Pakistan acquiesced to the Soviets, as Brzezinski believed they would without American aid, the dream could be fulfilled. It was time for the United States to step up and reemerge as the

---

[70] Summary of Conclusions: SCC Meeting on Soviet Moves in Afghanistan
[71] Reflections on Soviet Intervention in Afghanistan

world's leading anti-Soviet force. To stop the Soviets from making a major gain in the Cold War, it was "essential that the Afghani resistance continues." This would mean "more money and more arms shipments to the rebels, and some technical advice," as well as additional support for Pakistan. After a chill in the bilateral relationship with Pakistan over the nuclear human rights issues, it was time for a thaw. "Our security policy toward Pakistan cannot be dictated by our nonproliferation policy."[72]

In his letter to President Carter on the 26th, Brzezinski had recommended trying to involve the Chinese in the project to aid the Afghans. It remains unclear exactly when and how the two countries coordinated in the early stages of the war, but the Chinese did not need to wait for the Americans to start aiding the Afghans. After the failure of the United States to come to their aid in checking Soviet and Vietnamese hegemony in Southeast Asia, the Chinese were once again going to ensure that somebody was taking on the Soviets.

The Soviet invasion of Afghanistan infuriated the Chinese. On December 30, 1979, the Chinese government put out a strongly worded statement, summoned the Soviet ambassador, and tried to draw public attention to the hostile actions of the Soviets. According to the Chinese government:

> "The Soviet Union brazenly made a massive military invasion of Afghanistan, grossly interfering in its internal affairs. This armed intervention wantonly violates all norms of international relations. It not only encroaches upon the sovereignty and independence of Afghanistan but poses a grave threat to peace and security in Asia and the whole world. The Chinese Government vigorously condemns this hegemonistic action of the Soviet Union and firmly demands the cessation of this aggression and intervention in Afghanistan and withdrawal of all Soviet armed

---

[72] Ibid

force."

"The Soviet authorities have never had scruples in trying to realize their hegemonistic ambitions, but this time they have acted most outrageously. From pulling the strings and using surrogates, their method has escalated to direct involvement with their own troops, armed occupation of a sovereign country and change of its government by violent means. They have extended the use of the theory of limited sovereignty from their 'community of nations' to a non-aligned Islamic country of the third world."

"The Soviet Union claims its armed intervention in Afghanistan was undertaken in fulfillment at the request of the Afghan Government. This sophistry can fool no one. But this aggressor's logic warrants close attention. By its actions the Soviet Union shows that it is prepared to follow this logic and invade and occupy any country it wishes to invade and occupy. The Soviet Union itself acted according to this logic, and Vietnam, under Soviet instigation, used the same pretext for its armed invasion and occupation of Kampuchea [Cambodia]. How could the people of the world fail to be alerted by what is hidden behind the Soviet eagerness to sign 'treaties of friendship and cooperation'?"

"The current Soviet armed aggression in Afghanistan is a big show of Soviet hegemonism. People have come to see more clearly the source of the main threat to world peace and the true nature of this so called natural ally of the third world. They have come to see clearly that Soviet hegemonists are the most truculent and adventuristic, that the Soviet aggressive ambitions are unlimited, and that Soviet acts of aggression must be stopped effectively... the Chinese Government and people will work tirelessly with all countries and people who love peace and uphold justice to frustrate Soviet acts of aggression and expansion."[73]

This response was clearly designed to arouse leaders around the world into reflecting upon their own relationships with the Soviet Union. It was aimed at all nations who still maintained treaties of friendship and cooperation with the Soviet Union (China's treaty of

---

[73] "China Condemns Soviet Military Invasion of Afghanistan"

friendship with the Soviets would not officially expire until the next day). To nowhere though, was this pointed response more clearly aimed than at the United States. The 1971 Communiqué with the United States had established that the two would work together to fight against hegemonism in Asia. Now there was a clear and present effort to achieve hegemony by the Soviet Union, and it was time to act.

The Chinese media continued to launch a blistering attack on the Soviet Union over the coming weeks, accusing it of having orchestrated all of the Afghan coups since 1973 as part of 'the plan' to push southwards into Pakistan and Iran. The media put out the continued Chinese message to the world—that every nation was responsible for stopping the Soviet Union, as "hegemonists bent on expansion must be made to feel greater pressure exerted against them in order to stop their aggression and make them respect the basic principles concerning international relations."[74] The world needed to bloody the Soviets like the Chinese had bloodied Vietnam. Over the next few weeks, China continued to call on all peace-loving countries to strengthen, not relax, their joint efforts to punish the Soviet aggressors by applying sanctions against the Soviet Union, pushing back its expansionist offensive, and frustrating its global strategy. Brezhnev was compared to Hitler, and the Soviet Union was repeatedly characterized as a blood thirsty empire bent on global domination.[75] In a visit with Pennsylvania governor Richard Thornburg, Chinese Vice premier Li Xiannian outlined China's three principles for Afghanistan: the unconditional withdrawal of Soviet troops, the sovereignty of the Afghan people, and the justification for other countries (such as China) to aid the flourishing mujihadeen efforts to fight the Soviets.[76] From Beijing, the Soviet invasion

---

[74] "New Tsarist Challenge"
[75] "Aggressors Must Be Punished"

and the subsequent threat to both China and the global balance of power provided an excellent and necessary opportunity to bloody the Soviets.

It is still unclear exactly when the Chinese began to support the mujihadeen, and this will likely remain a permanent secret unless China chooses to open their intelligence archives. It is likely though, that by February of 1980, China was funneling money through Pakistan to arm the resistance. Up to three hundred Chinese military advisers lined Pakistan's border with Afghanistan, training rebels near Nawagai, Charsadda, Landi Kotal, and Peshawar.[77] In 1979, the CIA had helped to build and operate two "seismic and electronic facilities" in Xinjiang province, on the border with Afghanistan. Throughout the war, these bases would provide both the Chinese and American intelligence services with valuable intelligence on Russian troop movements and communications within Afghanistan.[78] Chinese weapons and ammunition had allowed the early resistance to rage against the Soviet Union, and China had quickly emerged as a serious provider for the mujihadeen.

In his 1980 State of the Union Address, President Carter outlined the threat facing the United States. The Soviet invasion, according to Carter, "could pose the most serious threat to the peace since the Second World War." While the world had expressed their opposition to the invasion, "verbal condemnation is not enough. The Soviet Union must pay a concrete price for their aggression." He went on to discuss troop deployments in the region, and committed the United States to the defense of Middle Eastern countries from the Soviet Union. It was time to get tough.[79]

---

[76] "Three Principles for Solution to Afghan Issue"
[77] Eftimiades, Nicholas 100-102
[78] Starr, S. Frederick 152-153
[79] Carter, Jimmy

President Carter followed through on his words. After spending the first half of his presidency building a reputation as a president who was unwilling to take a hard line towards the Soviet Union, Carter was about to surprise the world. Most of Carter's interactions with the CIA in his two years in office had revolved around gutting the agency following the scandal-ridden years preceding his administration. This made it all the more surprising that he would authorize what Gust Avrakotos, the CIA officer who would end up running the project from Langley, would call "the most comprehensive lethal findings ever commissioned, the equivalent of a presidential declaration of war."[80] Carter's gentle worldview had been permanently changed by the Soviet invasion. With the newly found thought that the Soviets might truly be an evil empire, President Carter sanctioned exports to the Soviet Union, committed the United States to war to prevent the possibility of Soviet troop movements in the Middle East, organized a boycott of the upcoming Moscow Olympics, and signed the findings that initiated Operation Cyclone, the project to fund the mujihadeen against the Soviet Union.[81]

Aid from the United States started off slow, but quickly picked up pace. The half million-dollar budget for the mujihadeen in 1979 grew to $10 million by 1982, all of which was routed through Pakistan and matched dollar for dollar by Saudi Arabia. The first shipments of weapons had been enough to arm just a thousand men, but within a year the CIA was arming around 30,000 men at a time.[82]

In May of 1981, Howard Hart arrived as the CIA station chief in Pakistan. Hart, who

---

[80] Crile, George 167
[81] Ibid 14-15
[82] Coll, Steve 79

had joined the CIA as the war in Vietnam was taking shape, was chosen to run the Afghanistan program because of his passion for weapons and paramilitary tactics. Hart had no real orders, as nobody in the CIA really understood the intricacies of Afghan politics. One standing order though, required that the program could not be traceable to the United States. As obvious as it was that the Americans were aiding the mujihadeen, the CIA, an agency facing outrage over its role in Nicaragua, wanted the program to be as covert as possible. The only weapons that they were allowed to ship in were weapons that the mujihadeen would already have access to, meaning either Soviet weapons that could be claimed to have been captured from Soviet forces, or old weapons that the British had left behind in their various incursions into Afghanistan. In the beginning, the rifle of choice was the Lee Enfield, a single shot World War One era British rifle that the CIA was able to purchase from Greece and India.[83] This single shot rifle was accurate against small groups of Soviet infantry, but was useless against tanks and helicopters. It would be extremely difficult though, to purchase the heavy weapons that the mujihadeen needed without giving up the covert nature of the operation.

    Even within the limits of the operation though, Hart was quite satisfied with his work. He had escalated a loosely affiliated series of village rebellions into a national war that was beginning to tie down the Soviet Union, and he had done so on a budget. Hart's intentions weren't even to defeat the Soviets, which was still seen as impossible. The point was merely to tie them down and make them bleed in Afghanistan for as long as possible, without endangering Pakistan. The Soviet Union was well aware that Pakistan was being used as a rear-base and as an armory for the mujihadeen. Pakistan's ISI and the CIA both had to ensure

---

[83] Coll, Steve 75-79

that the aid program was not large enough to cause the Soviets to invade Pakistan to clear the bases.[84]

It was in November of 1982 that the American project to aid the mujihadeen picked up its bizarre patron saint, Congressman Charlie Wilson. Wilson, an alcoholic who sat on the Defense Subcommittee of the House Appropriations Committee, was becoming a close personal friend of Zia-ul-Haq, and a closer friend of the mujihadeen. After visiting a refugee camp in Pakistan following a meeting with Zia, Wilson had become inspired. Taking on a nearly religious affinity for the cause in Afghanistan, his first meeting with Hart in Pakistan left Wilson astonished that the CIA was not doing more to try to win the war. Wilson, who understood neither the CIA strategy nor the limitations that the CIA was under, sought to use his committee seat to expand the war by forcing money down the pipeline for the Afghanistan project.

Wilson used his contacts in Egypt, Pakistan, and even Israel to ensure that a continuous flow of Soviet-designed weapons reached the mujihadeen. By 1983 Wilson had become a champion of the Afghan cause, and his time talking to refugees convinced him that the aid to the mujihadeen was simply not enough to be effective. One particular issue was that the Afghans lacked an effective anti-aircraft weapon to take on the Soviet Mi-24 helicopter, which was able to effectively bombard mujihadeen positions with impunity. Waking up to frequent nightmares about the Mi-24, Wilson desperately sought to provide the mujihadeen with the weaponry to take them on, but found the CIA uncooperative. In 1983, using his position on the Defense Appropriations subcommittee, Wilson personally ensured an earmark

---

[84] Crile, George 102-129

of an additional $40 million to the Afghan cause, with $17 million to go to anti-aircraft weapons, increasing the yearly budget from $10 million to $50 million.[85] The CIA had wanted a small, covert operation to make the Soviets bleed. Thanks to Congressman Wilson, they were forced to escalate.

The escalation of funds meant that the CIA needed to procure more and more Soviet weaponry, but they were finding it more and more difficult to do so. The Egyptian and Greeks, more eager to sell their outdated equipment than to win the war, were proving to be less and less reliable as the war went on. The black market was becoming a less than optimal destination to buy the weapons, as prices were increasing dramatically as the CIA diminished the stocks of weapons and ammunition that their sources could provide. It was Gust Avrakatos who realized that China, which was already funding the rebels, could serve as the perfect armory for the mujihadeen.

Joseph DeTrani, the CIA station chief in Beijing, met with his Chinese counterparts in 1984 to discuss the possibility of using the might of the Chinese arms manufacturing industry to turn the tide against the Soviets. The Chinese arms soon stared to flow. Millions of dollars' worth of AK-47s, machine guns, and rocket propelled grenades, now being paid for by the Americans, begun to find their ways from Shanghai to Karachi in predictable and steady quantities. The biggest effect that the Chinese production had was on the price of weapons. Chinese production managed to bring the cost of a black market AK-47 down from the $139 that the CIA was paying the Egyptians to under $100. The price of a mine dropped from $500 to $75. Of the $50 Million that the CIA was spending in 1984, $38 million, a full 76 percent,

---

[85] Crile, George 215

was going to buy weapons from China.[86] China would also be a major supplier of the much needed mules (the mountainous terrain and poor infrastructure made mules the optimal vehicles to deliver weapons into Afghanistan) that would travel along the Karakoram highway into Pakistan before crossing into Afghanistan.[87] Military-owned factories in China were soon working at full capacity to supply these weapons to the war effort, and the costs of buying Chinese weapons would average out to about $100 million a year.[88]

The Chinese weaponry had allowed the CIA and the matching Saudi donors to get far more bang for their buck, helping to dramatically escalate the war, which was now being fully supported by President Reagan. The Americans though, were not the only ones expanding their aid to the mujihadeen. Between 1980 and 1984, before the CIA had begun consulting with China, $400 million worth of arms had already been sent from China to Pakistan for the mujihadeen. After the CIA began to coordinate with China, China continued to unilaterally support the mujihadeen by escalating the supply of light weapons into heavy weapons, including 107mm and 122mm artillery pieces, 130mm anti-aircraft guns, along with other heavy weaponry. In 1985, China opened the first training camps in Xinjiang, where the People's Liberation Army directly trained Afghans in the use of weapons, the applications of propaganda, and combat.[89]

As both the United States and China, along with their Saudi funders and Pakistani hosts, were escalating their efforts, it was becoming increasingly obvious that these efforts were working. Soviet troops were being killed in increasingly large numbers, Soviet tanks

---

[86] Ibid 268-269
[87] Starr, S. Frederick 153
[88] Tomsen, Peter 266-267
[89] Eftimiades, Nicholas 100-102

were being blown to pieces, and the first helicopters were being shot down. Americans saw this as an opportunity to double down, however the political strategy coming from Beijing was changing. With the Soviets bogged down in Afghanistan, Beijing's view to the north was far less frightening, and even as Chinese arms shipments were escalating, the Chinese sought to begin a diplomatic thaw with the Soviets.[90] The Chinese were seeking closer ties with the Soviet Union, and in 1985, a visit to Moscow by Chinese Premier Yao Yilin would culminate with a trade and economic cooperation agreement between the China and the Soviet Union.[91] In the past China had used closer ties with the United States to rebalance the global balance of power against the Soviet Union. Sensing that the balance of power had now been shifted against the Soviet Union, Beijing now wanted to give the Soviets some extra weight on the scale.

President Reagan did not bother himself by fretting over the regional balance of power in Asia. Reagan wanted to put the wounded bear out of its misery. In his 1985 State of the Union Address, Reagan made it clear that the United States would support fighters "on every continent, from Afghanistan to Nicaragua—to defy Soviet-supported aggression and secure rights which have been ours from birth."[92] In 1985, Reagan publicly met with various mujihadeen leaders including the famed Abdul Haq,[93] publicly acknowledged US support for the mujihadeen,[94] and signed NSDD 166, which directed the CIA to "Improve the intelligence support to our covert action program... utilize intelligence to focus increased effort on the

---

[90] Kissinger, Henry 323-327
[91] Ibid 327
[92] Reagan, Ronald
[93] Kaplan, Robert D 94
[94] Crile, George 209

systematic exploitation of Soviet sensitivities and vulnerabilities... [and] improve the military effectiveness of the Afghan resistance."[95] Another round of escalation was in order.

In the spring of 1986, covertness for Operation Cyclone took a backseat to combat effectiveness. With the United States already running over $750 million a year (along with a matching contribution from the Saudis) to Chinese weapons shipments and Pakistani training camps for the mujihadeen, the CIA decided that it was be willing to allow the use of an American weapon to finally fix the Mi-24 problem that Congressman Wilson was obsessed with. In the spring of 1986, the first Stinger missiles arrived in the hands of the Pakistanis and their Afghan trainees.[96]

On September 26, 1986, a group of mujihadeen fighting under the banner of the Hezb-i-Islam Gulbuddin (HIG) group moved into the perimeter of a Soviet airfield outside of Jalalabad. Four Stingers were fired, and three Mi-24s burst into flames over the skies of Nangarhar before crashing down to earth. The Stingers, which cost between $60,000-$70,000 each, had just brought down $30 million worth of Soviet helicopters.[97]

The introduction of the Stinger represented another major escalation by the United States. For the first time, Afghans were fighting the Soviets with weapons that were easily traceable to the United States. By this point though, the CIA had already determined that if the Soviets, who were well aware that Pakistan was being used as a major hub for the arms movements, hadn't already invaded Pakistan, they weren't willing to do so after another escalation.[98]

---

[95] U.S. Policy, Programs, and Strategy in Afghanistan
[96] Ibid 419-421
[97] Ibid 437, 270
[98] Ibid 419

The Stingers were effective, and when they were combined with other anti-aircraft weapons being purchased from Eastern European countries or shipped in from China, helicopter pilots had reason to be afraid for the first time in the war. With 70% of Stingers fired successfully bringing down a Soviet aircraft, Russian pilots were now flying too high to be the effective force multiplier that they had once been.[99]

By the time that the Soviet Union fully withdrew from Afghanistan in 1989, as much as $10 billion of American aid, matched in its entirety by Saudi Arabia, had been spent in Afghanistan.[100] It remains extremely opaque how much China had exerted in the Afghan effort, but it is perfectly clear that Chinese contributions were essential to keep the war going. In a joint covert operation that would have been unthinkable just a decade before the operations began, the United States and the People's Republic of China had helped to kill approximately 28,000 Soviet soldiers and to cripple the Soviet Union.[101]

The covert war in Afghanistan has, to the public, become a lesson in unintended consequences. The mountains of Afghanistan attracted thousands of Arab fighters, including Osama Bin Laden, Abdullah Azzam, and Ayman al-Zawahiri, who would found al-Qaeda in Afghanistan in the late 1980s.[102] The decision to allow the entirety of American aid to flow through Pakistan led to the rise of an ISI favorite, Gulbuddin Hekmatyar, the mujihadeen commander whose HIG organization fired the first stinger missiles, and who is now known as one of the top commanders fighting the United States in Afghanistan.[103] The proliferation of

---

[99] Ibid 437-438
[100] Wawro, Geoffrey 385
[101] Crile, George 511
[102] Wawro, Geoffrey. 389
[103] Mashal, Mujib

heavy weaponry led to the brutal series of civil wars that allowed the Taliban to rise to power between 1994 and 1996. Stinger missiles ended up in Iran,[104] and Afghanistan would become the safe haven for terrorists that allowed the attacks on American embassies in 1998 and the attacks of September 11 to be carried out. Jalaluddin Haqqani, who Charlie Wilson had once described as "goodness personified,"[105] went on to use the Haqqani network that he built during the war against the Soviets to carry out an ongoing wave of attacks against American and Afghan National Army troops and property. The radicalization of both Afghans and Arabs in Saudi-built madrassahs in the tribal regions of Pakistan will provide terrorist organizations with foot soldiers and commanders for years to come. The radicalization has also spread to Xinjiang's Uyghur Muslims, and the anarchy that emerged in Afghanistan allowed for Uyghur terrorist organizations like the East Turkestan Independence Movement to train and recruit in Afghanistan.[106] The largest covert war in history was certainly not without its blowback.

One of the biggest causes and effects of the operation though, was the culmination of two decades of diplomatic efforts between the United States and China. In 1954, the Soviet Union and the People's Republic of China nearly engaged nuclear war against the United States. Following the Sino-Soviet split in the early 1960s and the Nixon/Kissinger visits in the 1970s, China slowly began to shift its weight to balance out the great Cold War power struggle between the United States and the Soviet Union.

In 1979, the view from Beijing was terrifying. The Soviet Union was a grave threat to China, massing troops on the border and surrounding the Chinese with their surrogates in

---

[104] Coll, Steve 33
[105] Crile, George 521
[106] Brown, Vahid, and Don Rassler 111-113

Central Asia, India, and Southeast Asia. Under President Carter, the United States had been unable to balance out the Soviet Union, and the Chinese under Deng Xiaoping realized that they needed to devote their full weight against the Soviets. A short war with Vietnam helped the Chinese to diminish the threat from fellow communists in Southeast Asia, but the Soviet invasion of Afghanistan in December of 1979 gave the Chinese and the Americans another opportunity to weaken the Soviet Union. Over the next ten years, the two once-hostile powers came together to fund the largest covert war in the history of the world, leaving the corpse of another great empire in the mountains of Afghanistan. While the two countries did not see the world through the same lens, and even fundamentally disagreed with the direction that they should take with the Soviet Union, it is clear that both countries were vital players in the effort to win the war in Afghanistan for the mujihadeen. Through the war in Afghanistan, a new era in relations between the United States and China had been crafted, one in which the ideological fervor that had once divided them was replaced by a realist geopolitical relationship between two great powers, and the rift between the PRC and the Soviet Union was pried open as Chinese aid to the mujihadeen continued to flow throughout the conflict. Perhaps Asia was simply too crowded for two major land powers.

A Hundred Years Added to my Life

Afghanistan in the 1970s was, as it has been for much of the last few centuries, a collection of tribes weakly bound to the Kabul government by force, wealth, and familial ties. Afghanistan lacked a strong and centralized state capable of taming its tribes or nearing monopolization of security, and the Kabul government instead relied on the utilization of tribal authorities to extend Kabul's rule over the rest of the country. With a society that was largely illiterate, economically underdeveloped, and deeply divided across ethnic and tribal lines, Afghanistan constantly seemed to be on the brink of fracturing into a state of total anarchy at any moment, and the insurgency facing Kabul throughout the 1970s only served to enhance the risk of a full scale civil war. These fractures within Afghan Society brought the Pakistanis into a series of repeatedly failed efforts to impose Islam as a political identity to eclipse Afghanistan and Pakistan's ethnic divisions, and eventually led to the Soviet Invasion.

Both the Soviet Union and Pakistan, countries that stood to Afghanistan's north and southeast, were threatened by the spillover from violent fallout that followed the overthrow of King Zahir Shah in 1973. For Pakistan, the overthrow of Zahir and the assumption of power by his cousin and former Prime Minister, Daoud Khan Mohammad, served as a threat capable of spreading Afghanistan's ethnic divisions across the border and unraveling the state of Pakistan itself. Pakistan responded by seeking to unite its people and secure the state by appealing to the lowest common denominator—Islam. As perhaps the only force for unity within Afghanistan and Pakistan, the Pakistani government embarked upon a deliberate strategy of supporting increasingly radical forms of political Islam in the hopes that it could provide a level of unification to the long-divided Afghans and protect Pakistan from its own internal schisms.

The Soviet Union, fearful that the divisions within Afghanistan would provide the United States and the People's Republic of China with an opportunity to establish a foothold under the Soviet Union's soft underbelly, attempted to support the imposition of an altogether different type of political ideology, communism. By training Afghan Communists in Soviet universities and supporting Communist leaders, Moscow ensured that communism would be a potent force within Afghanistan's universities, political class, and military.

The introduction of communism into Afghanistan did more to unite the Afghans under the banner of Islam than any previous campaign by Pakistan had ever managed to do. The spread of a godless and radical political ideology into Afghanistan inspired strong blowback, tentatively uniting the Islamists in both Kabul's universities and the untamed hinterlands of Afghanistan's tribal corridors against the perceived influx of communist control over their lives. While it by no means healed the various ethnic, tribal, and personal divisions that encompass Afghan society, the introduction of Communism and the subsequent backlash temporarily eclipsed the intra-Islamic feuds and turned a series of long-running tribal conflicts into a universal ideological battle for the future of the Islamic world.

The fallout from Pakistan's Islam-over-Tribe strategy has had and continues to have widespread fallout well beyond Afghanistan and Pakistan. To jihadists fighting local battles across the Islamic World, including al-Qaeda founders and leaders Zawahiri, bin Laden, and Azzam, the strategy that culminated in the battle for Afghanistan is applicable to the entire Muslim world, both at its core and at its fringes. The foreign fighters that flocked to fight in Afghanistan from around the globe came from different ideological backgrounds, different national struggles, and different organizations, yet they all came under the belief that the global struggle against the apostate forces of communism in Afghanistan had eclipsed their divisions.

Throughout the mid-1980s, the fighting between mujihadeen leaders Ahmed Shah Massoud and Gulbuddin Hekmatyar emerged as a war within a war. The ethnic conflict between the Tajik Massoud and Hekmatyar, the ISI-backed Pashtun, continued well after the Soviets pulled out and has yet to be fully resolved, awaiting a potential resurgence following the American withdrawal from Afghanistan. What was built in the mountains of Afghanistan though, was a network of jihadists that, despite internal feuding, was able to find compromise around different ethnicities, different Islamic ideologies, and even different languages in the search for common ground against a highly visible enemy. Arabs, Turks, Uighurs, Chechens, Deobandis, Wahhabis, Muslim Brothers, and supporters of Egyptian Islamic Jihad, among the multitude of other ways to divide the jihadi movement, were able to put aside their differences under the flag of jihad and coalesce around the newly emerged al-Qaeda organization. The internal schisms that have plagued the al-Qaeda movement from its inception though, continue to play out on the battlefields of Syria as the Islamic State in Iraq and al-Sham battles against Jabhat al-Nusra, despite the fact that the two groups both emerged as regional al-Qaeda franchises.

The internal divisions within the Islamic world were not healed by the Soviet-Afghan War. Even the internal divisions within Afghanistan began to show through early in the conflict and continued unabated well after the Soviets had pulled out. What emerged from Afghanistan though, was a rapid expansion of Pakistan's Islam-over-Tribe strategy, a strategy that continues to play out as Kazakhs, Chechens, North Africans, Malaysians, and Saudis, among others, join their Arab Syrian and Iraqi brethren on the battlefields of Syria and Iraq. The fallout from the Soviet-Afghan War was the culmination of years of deliberate strategy pursued by both Pakistan and the Soviet Union, and the blowback will remain with the world for years to come.

4. The Shah Goes to Rome, Never Comes Back

Jalaluddin Haqqani was outgunned by the Soviet forces that moved through Afghanistan with near impunity. Calls for jihad were pouring out of Afghanistan's mosques and madrassahs[107] and militias were being raised to fight the intruders, but the Soviet military power was overwhelming most attempts to defend all but the most fortified and isolated positions. Even with foreign aid beginning to trickle in, the plight of the Afghans in their struggle against a global superpower seemed impossible. Facing impossible odds, Haqqani put out a call for help:

> "Even though the revolutionary fighters are great in number, this does not mean that the revolution should close its doors to those who wish to participate in the Jihad. Scores of volunteers from various parts of the world are coming to use to join the ranks of the mujihadeen. They are doing so of their own volition. If the Islamic world truly wants to support and help us, let it permit its men and young men to join our ranks. There is a tendency in most of the Islamic countries which wish to help us to present aid and food as at kind of Jihad. Some even think that this is the best kind of Jihad. This, however, does not absolve the Muslim of the duty to offer himself for the Jihad."[108]

This pronouncement, made under the threat of communist occupation of an Islamic heartland, began a chain of events that transformed the Jihadi movement around the globe.

Abdullah Azzam, who arrived in 1980 to answer the call of Haqqani, was not the first foreigner to arrive at the training camps being run by Haqqani—that honor likely goes to Abu'l-Walid al-Masri[109] (real name Mustafa Hamid), an Egyptian journalist and future al-Qaeda strategist who traveled to Afghanistan in the summer of 1979. Azzam though, would go

---

[107] Lamb, Christina 84
[108] Brown, Vahid, and Don Rassler 62
[109] Brown, Vahid, and Don Rassler 64

on to make a name for himself as perhaps the most influential Islamic cleric of the entire conflict, using his Fatwas to motivate thousands of Muslim youths to leave their homes behind and to redefine Jihad in the mountains of Afghanistan. By the time that the Soviets had pulled their troops out of Afghanistan in 1989, the fallout from the rise of the political Jihadi movement was on the path to fundamentally altering the political realities of much of the Muslim world. It is perhaps unfitting of this grandiose narrative then, that such a conflict has its roots in a tribal timber dispute.

Back in September of 1959, a tribal feud had broken out in Afghanistan's Paktia province, home of the Haqqanis. The rival Zadran and Mangal tribes were involved in a rather typical dispute—two tribes with a long running feud fighting over a piece of land that both sides needed to survive through the agricultural off-season—and the dispute would have remained typical had it not been for the response from Prime Minister Daoud Khan, whose Pashtun nationalism put him at the forefront of an existential tug of war between Afghanistan and Pakistan.[110] With the fighting between the two tribes dragging on, Daoud, cousin of King Zahir Shah, sent his army to Paktia to back the weaker Zadrans, leaving the Mangals to flee into Pakistan.[111] Daoud had attempted to manipulate the Pashtun tribal system to quiet a local dispute, but he would soon find that he had opened a much larger conflict.

The Mangals who fled over the Durand Line and into Pakistan were welcomed with open arms by the government of Pakistan, the leadership of which was deeply afraid of Daoud's ties to the Pashtun nationalist movement. In 1947, as the British were pulling out of India, many Pashtun leaders, including Daoud, had coalesced around the nationalist Ghaffar

---

[110] Ibid 35
[111] Ibid

Khan. Khan had been propagating the idea that the British pullout offered Afghanistan the chance to renegotiate the 1894 Durand Line and to claim Pakistan's Pashtun tribal belt for Afghanistan and unite the Pashtuns under one flag, a concept that was popular among Kabul's political elite.[112] These Pashtun nationalists quickly became one of many deep existential threats to the newly formed Pakistan, which, plagued by the spectre of Pakistan's Pashtun, Bengali, Sindh, and Baluch enclaves, viewed ethnic nationalism as a force that could be manipulated to permanently dismantle Pakistan.

The Pashtunistan debate between Afghanistan and Pakistan would flare early and often. Afghanistan voted against Pakistan's inclusion in the United Nations over the belief that the border issue had yet to be resolved,[113] and convened a *loya jirga* [a grand tribal gathering] to formally repudiate the idea that the Durand Line could stand as an international border.[114] Pakistan would spend the next three decades routinely raising the issue in meetings with American envoys in attempts to prevent large-scale American aid to Afghanistan,[115] and even went as far as to close its borders with Afghanistan over the issue in 1949.[116]

Pakistan's objections to American aid to Afghanistan over the Pashtunistan issue were ultimately a success, and the failure of the United States to seriously engage with Kabul, combined with Pakistan's border closures, forced Zahir Shah and Daoud to seek help from the Soviet Union. By 1954, the two countries had signed their first mutual agreements, which included economic aid in the form of loans, grain, and energy pipelines, and the Soviet Union

---

[112] Haqqani, Husain 29-31
[113] Ibid
[114] Bradsher, Henry S 21
[115] Haqqani, Husain 35
[116] Bradsher, Henry S 21

began to openly support Afghanistan in the Pashtunistan dispute, leading to a flare-up that again closed the Afghanistan-Pakistan border.[117] As it had in 1949, the border closure forced Afghanistan to move closer to the Soviet Union, further terrifying Pakistan. The prospect of the Soviet Union, which was also courting closer ties with India, serving as the backbone of an Afghan-Soviet-Indian alliance against Pakistan was, to the ever-paranoid Pakistanis, a nightmare situation. When Daoud sent his troops to Paktia in 1959, Pakistan's existential fear turned the situation into an international incident.

Pakistan, in an attempt to do away with the Pashtunistan issue, immediately began to aid the Mangal tribesmen who had fled across Pakistan's Northwest border. Pakistan skillfully used its media and mosque propaganda networks to cast the issue as one not between two tribes, but between the forces of apostasy and the forces of Islam. Playing on Daoud's ties to the Soviet Union, the violation of the presumed autonomy of the highland Pashtuns, and westernizing reforms that Daoud had previously attempted to implement, Pakistan was able to manipulate Pashtun tribes into open revolt against Daoud, forcing him to use troops in Kandahar, Paktia, and Khost,[118][119] where he was being confronted by Pakistan-backed rebels.

Daoud responded by sending troops over the border. He hoped to quell the use of Pakistan's disputed tribal areas as a rear base for anti-government activity, leading to another round of border closures from Pakistan, this time lasting for four years. With customs duties from the Afghanistan-Pakistan border accounting for a full forty percent of the Kabul government's revenue,[120] the border closures crippled Afghanistan's economy and further

---

[117] Ibid 23-25
[118] Ibid 30
[119] Brown, Vahid, and Don Rassler 35
[120] Bradsher, Henry S 33

pushed Kabul into a dependence on Moscow.[121] Even with Soviet aid though, the border closures soon began to cripple Afghanistan's economy and by 1963, the worsening situation forced Daoud to resign.[122] With Afghanistan in the midst of a political crisis, Zahir Shah convened a *loya jirga* which introduced a new constitution. This short-lived constitution banned any members of the royal family from serving at the cabinet level, a clear way of closing the door behind Daoud.[123] After serving as a rallying cry against Daoud, Islam had proven itself to be a potent force in Afghan politics, but the battle between ethnic nationalism and political Islam in South Asia was far from being settled.

The Pakistani government had skillfully maneuvered against Daoud and the Pashtun independence movement by undercutting the tribal component of the conflict and instead framing it as one against the forces of apostasy and atheism. As a country lacking a nationalist force to hold itself together, Pakistan needs to continuously use Islam as a means to quell the tribal or national movements that have plagued Pakistan from its birth. Daoud's nationalism had offered Pakistani policy makers a chance to use the call to fulfill Islamic duties as a national rallying cry, uniting the needs of the Pakistani state with the needs of a resurgent Islamic movement. This skillful maneuvering had also succeeded in aligning Daoud, who was not an ideological communist, with the communists in the Soviet Union and within Afghanistan. Pakistan had managed to build ties with the Pashtun tribes which straddle the Durand Line and to move them away from the Durrani monarchy, which would offer Pakistan the upper hand in any future conflict in Afghanistan. The removal of Daoud though, did not

---

[121] Ibid 30-31
[122] Ibid
[123] Lamb, Christina 130

end the existential nightmares over India, Pashtunistan, and a potential Afghan-Soviet-Indian alliance that kept Pakistan's leadership up at night. Such an existential nightmare would persist until it had turned the region into both the focal point of the Cold War and the focal point of a Sunni Islamic revival.

Jalaluddin Haqqani, the man who would soon find himself near the center of a global Jihadist movement, was, throughout the 1950s, living a relatively normal life for a highland Pashtun living on the Durand Line. Born as the son of a moderately wealthy landowner in rural Afghanistan's feudal system, Haqqani grew up as one of many sons of the Zadran tribe which, in a reflection of divisions of Pashtun society as a whole, has a long history of fighting for autonomy against the modernist reforms of the Durrani Dynasty.

The Durranis, who came to power in 1747, first established themselves in the lowland plains of Kandahar before Timur Shah, the second Durrani King, moved to Kabul in 1772 in an attempt to escape from the warring Pashtun tribes of the southern valley.[124] While the Durrani Dynasty has often been characterized (correctly) by constant infighting, civil war, and intra-familial murder, the Durrani dynasty has also been home to a number of rulers who have attempted to invoke western-style reforms in an effort to modernize the country. The Zadran tribe, in the manner that one would expect rural mountain-people to respond to attempts by urban city dwellers to impose social change, often found themselves in open revolt against reforms ranging from King Aminullah's attempts to force Afghans to wear western clothing[125] to Zahir and Daoud's attempts to increase the rights of women.[126]

---

[124] Dalrymple, William 10-11
[125] Lamb, Christina 125-126
[126] Brown, Vahid, and Don Rassler 34

Jalaluddin, like many of the young tribal Pashtuns who could afford the privilege, marked 1963 by crossing the border into Pakistan to attend Dar al-'Ulum Haqqaniyya.[127] Located about 30 miles southeast of Peshawar, the Haqqaniyya madrassa, also known as Jamia Haqqaaniyya, is one of the foremost madrassahs of the Deobandi movement, and the position of many alumni at the forefront of the Pashtun Jihadi movement has led to the nickname "Jihad University."[128]

Founded in 1947 by Abdul Haq (unrelated to the Kabul mujihadeen commander of the same name), Jamia Haqqaniyya is modeled off of Haq's alma mater, Dar al-'Ulum Deoband, the Indian madrassah from which the Deobandi school of Islam originated.[129] Deobandism, a school of thought that goes back to 17th century India, was founded to purify Islam from the mystical Sufi practices that were commonplace of the era[130] and to instead preach a literalistic interpretation of the Quran. Like Wahhabism, Deobandism is essentially an attempt to restore Islam to the golden age that it experienced at the time of the prophet by purifying it to its roots.[131] Born out of opposition to British rule,[132] the anti-colonial Deobandi School quickly spread throughout Asia, catching on with disaffected Muslims eager to cleanse Islam of Western, Hindu, Shia, and other apostate influences. By the second decade of the 20th Century, the Deobandis had become a serious political force among the highland Pashtuns of Eastern Afghanistan and Northwestern Pakistan,[133] and by the time that Jalaluddin Haqqani

---

[127] Ibid 38
[128] Lamb, Christina 84
[129] Brown, Vahid, and Don Rassler 38
[130] Haroon, Sana 48
[131] Lamb, Christina 97
[132] Nasr, Vali 101
[133] Haroon, Sana 49-51

enrolled in Jamia Haqqaniyya, the Deobandis had reformed into a tightly knit group that, as a united bloc, had formed a political party and elected representatives to Pakistan's National Assembly.[134] While not yet an altogether significant force in Pakistani politics, the Deobandi School was emerging as a restorationist ideological faction that could unite the regressive highland Pashtuns under one ideological banner, and Jamia Haqqaniyya was emerging as a key school of the Deobandi movement, graduating approximately a third of all Deobandi clerics between 1966 and 1985.[135]

As the highland Pashtuns were centering their religious revival around the Haqqaniyya madrassa near Peshawar, a separate ideological battle was brewing at Kabul University. As Zahir Shah's ineffectual reforms failed to strengthen the hand of the Kabul royalists, two factions, the urban Islamists and the Afghan Communists, were fighting for control of the post-Durrani future that both parties foresaw emerging out of the weakened monarchy.

Zahir Shah's new constitution had allowed the development of political parties, and the communists were quick to take advantage. Founded in early 1965 by a handful of "comrades" that included two future Afghan presidents, Nur Mohammaed Taraki and Babrak Karmal, the People's Democratic Party of Afghanistan (PDPA), also known as the Afghan Communist Party, was quick to recruit from Kabul's Universities and high schools. By the end of 1965, they had emerged as a significant and influential part of Kabul's political sphere, infiltrating and organizing local strikes, organizing widespread protests that would lead to the resignation of Prime Minister Yousef, and were preparing to launch "Khalq," one of the six officially sanctioned newspapers being produced in Kabul.[136]

---

[134] Ibid 57-62
[135] Brown, Vahid, and Don Rassler 39

The Soviet Union, as part of its relations with the Daoud government, had been bringing Afghans to study at Moscow's universities since at least 1955, educating them as communists and training them with Soviet political and propaganda techniques.[137] The Soviets recruited Taraki, the first leader of the PDPA, for a forty-eight day stay in the Soviet Union, treating the head of the newly formed communist party as if he was the Afghan head of state, and built ties that would eventually propel him to emerge with the title.[138] The Soviet support for the PDPA continued well into the 1970s, a decade marked by coups, revolution, and all-out war in Afghanistan.

Opposing the Communists were the Kabul Islamists, a group of mostly lowland Pashtuns (with notable exceptions that include the highland Hekmatyar and the Tajik Massoud), who, like the highland Pashtuns at Jamia Haqqaniyya, were beginning to embrace a hardline approach to Islam as a political identity. Unlike the Deobandi Highlanders though, the urban Islamists, whose ranks included the future mujihadeen leaders Gulbuddin Hekmatyar, Ahmed Shah Massoud, Burhanuddin Rabbani, and Rasul Sayyaf, among others, did not pick up a literalist interpretations of the Quran, but instead took on the texts and ideology of the Muslim Brotherhood.[139][140]

The Kabul Islamists, unlike their Deobandi brethren, were statists. They did not seek autonomy from the state or its dissolution, but instead sought to replace it with an Islamic State based on Sharia Law. In a bizarre mirror of the Afghan Communists, early publications

---

[136] Bradsher, Henry S 43-49
[137] Ibid 25
[138] Ibid 47-48
[139] Brown, Vahid, and Don Rassler 36-38
[140] Coll, Steve 113-114

by the Kabul Islamists, perhaps in an attempt to appeal to the common Kabul resident, spoke of societal degradation and class warfare as their primary grievances against the Durranis. As Soviet-backed communists grew more powerful, the Islamists turned more radical as the two ideological factions fought for support from the growing politically active population, and the two sides began to openly fight on the streets of Kabul. Combining their distaste for the state with the growing fear that the communists were becoming more powerful within the state, the Kabul Islamists declared a jihad against the Durrani line in 1965.[141]

The jihad declared by the Kabul Islamists was not without controversy in clerical circles. Mainstream definitions of jihad, perhaps because they were being propagated by clerics with ties to various states, had maintained that the idea of jihad as an obligation was to be used for purely defensive purposes, to be used only when Islam had a clear oppressor and all other options were off the table. The 13th/14th century Islamic scholar Ibn Taymiyyah, today considered to be the father of the doctrine of jihad and a heavy influence on both Abdullah Azzam and Osama bin Laden, among other influential Jihadis, glorifies the practice of jihad himself, but takes a much more limited approach than the Kabul Islamists were taking. While he maintains that jihad "is the best voluntary [religious] act that man can perform... better than the hajj (greater pilgrimage) and the 'umrah (lesser pilgrimage), than voluntary salaah and voluntary fasting,"[142] Taymiyyah believes that such an act should always be defensive. Explaining his views, Taymiyyah writes that:

> "We may only fight those who fight us when we want to make the religion of Allah victorious...
> This means that, although there is evil and abomination in killing, there is greater evil and

---

[141] Olesen, Asta 231-233
[142] Ibn Taymiyyah, Taqi Ad-Din Ahmad 25

abomination in the persecution of the unbelievers. Now, the unbelief of those who do not hinder the Muslims from establishing the religion of Allah is only prejudicial to themselves...So the latter [form of Jihad] consists in defense of the religion, of things that are inviolable, and of lives. Therefore it is fighting out of necessity. The former [type of Jihad], however, is voluntary fighting in order to propagate the religion, to make it triumph and to intimidate the enemy, such as was the case with the expedition to Tabuk and the like."[143]

Taymiyyah leaves the nuances of his words open to interpretation, but he clearly states that, as long as Muslims are able to practice their religion without persecution, a fight against the perceived enemies of Islam cannot be considered a religious obligation. The Kabul Islamists though, were more heavily inspired by the Egyptian scholar Sayyid Qutb than by Taymiyyah. Qutb, an educator-turned radical who was jailed in 1954 after orchestrating a plot to assassinate Egyptian President Gamel Nasser, wrote *Milestones* (also known as *Signposts*) from his jail cell, releasing it in 1964, just two years before his 1966 execution. Qutb's writing is best known as inspirational material for the Muslim Brotherhood, but it also served as a blueprint for the Kabul Islamists as they fought in the upcoming ideological clashes in Afghanistan.

The purpose of Jihad, as told by Qutb, "is to secure complete freedom for every man throughout the world by releasing him from servitude to other human beings so that he may serve his God."[144] Sensing that he was living in the age of an Islamic revival, Qutb sought for *Milestones* to spell out how an influx of young, politically motivated Muslims could turn their zeal into the type of force for political change that Qutb had failed to accomplish in his own life. Qutb, believing that an ideal Islamic society should be ruled by God and legislated by

---

[143] Ibid 25-35
[144] Qutb, Sayyid, and Badrul S. Hasan 44

Islamic scholars interpreting the Quran, believed that any and all legal systems not based on such a system were an inherent affront to Muslims and an inherent attack on Islam, and therefore, a defensive Jihad against these systems was necessary. Doing away with the notion of defensive Jihad being reserved for direct attacks by non-Muslims, Qutb writes:

> "If we insist on calling Islamic Jihad a defensive movement, then we must change the meaning of the word 'defense' and mean by it 'the defense of man' against all those elements which limit his freedom. These elements take the form of beliefs and concepts, as well as of political systems, based on economic, racial, or class distinctions."[145]

To Qutb, perhaps in a reflection of his own choices to fight the Egyptian government, freedom from man-made political systems is the ultimate goal of the Islamic revival, and any government that does not seek to impose a Sharia-based rule is a target. Only when such governments were overthrown could men be free from the inherently oppressive rule of man.

It makes sense then that, following Qutb, the Kabul Islamists turned their anger upon the Durrani monarchy, yet these Muslim student activists, perhaps too distracted by their fight against the rising communist movement, failed to achieve any real political power. The networking and organization building done during this period failed to unite the Kabul Islamists in any meaningful sense, as ethnic, tribal, and personal disputes between these men divided them far more than their common ideology could unite them. These divisions were perhaps another warning sign to Pakistan, whose ISI was closely watching the situation in Kabul, that political Islam was not yet developed as enough of a force to overcome the complicated forces tearing the Islamists apart.

The Islamists were not the only ideological faction struggling to maintain unity. By

---

[145] Ibid 37

1968, the PDPA had split into two groups, the Parchams, led by Karmal, and the Khalqis, led by Tarkaki. Tarkai, the Soviet favorite, maintained that the overthrow of the monarchy was the desired communist goal, while Karmal suggested working through the reformist king to achieve a socialist society. As both sides organized themselves, strikes, protests, and subversive newsletters became the normal state of Kabul society as the weakening monarchy failed to effectively reform Afghanistan's dysfunctional political system.[146]

As early as 1970, the Parcham faction, believing that it needed to work within Afghanistan's political system to enact change, had begun to recruit officers in the military. These officers, some of whom were trained in the Soviet Union under the Soviet education program, tended to have close personal relationships with Daoud, who had once been their defense minister. By July of 1972, Daoud was working with these Moscow oriented officers on a personal project of his.[147]

On July 17, 1973, Afghans awoke to find that the monarchy had been dissolved. Zahir Shah, who was traveling in Italy for a medical procedure, had been deposed, leaving him stranded in Rome. Using the Parcham military officers who he had been conspiring with, Daoud and his men surrounded key military, police, radio, and other government installations, seizing Kabul's power centers for themselves.[148] The royal family was rounded up, loaded onto transport planes, and sent out of the country, never to return.[149]

---

[146] Bradsher, Henry S 43-49
[147] Ibid 56
[148] Ibid
[149] Lamb, Christina 111-115

5. Exodus

Afghanistan's history is complete with a dizzying array of royalty murdering royalty for money, power, revenge, or simply a result of personality clash. Daoud's coup though, was widely and incorrectly perceived to be based not just on personality, but on ideology. The use of the Parcham communists in the coup had initially emboldened those who sought to establish a communist state in Afghanistan, while horrifying those who sought the establishment of an Islamic state. By 1973 Kabul Islamists were openly murdering communists in the streets,[150] and were thus horrified by the notion that a communist had come to power. The Islamists immediately accelerated efforts to subvert the state. When it came to the prospect of living under communism, the Kabul Islamists mirrored Sayyid Qutb whose commentary on the issue claimed that:

> "All Societies existing in the world today are *jahili* [the state of ignorance of the guidance from God.] Included among these is the communist society, first because it denies the existence of God Most High and believes that the universe was created by 'matter' or by 'nature', while all man's activities and his history has been created by 'economics or 'the means of production'; second, because the way of life it adopts is based on submission to the Communist Party and not to God. A proof of this is that in all communist countries the Communist Party has full control and leadership Furthermore, the practical consequence of this ideology is that the basic needs of human beings are considered identical with those of animals, that is food and drink, clothing, shelter, and sex. It deprives people of their spiritual needs, which differentiate human beings from animals. Foremost among these is belief in God and the freedom to adopt and to proclaim this faith. Similarly, it deprives people of their freedom to express individuality, which is a very special human characteristic. The individuality of a person is expressed in various ways, such as

---

[150] Coll, Steve 114

private property, the choice of work and the attainment of specialization in work, and expression in various art forms; and it distinguishes him from animals or from machines. The communist ideology and the communist system reduces the human being to the level of an animal or even to the level of a machine."[151]

To Qutb, the communist society that many believed Daoud was imposing on Afghanistan was among the worst systems of political organization in existence. Not only did the Communist society consolidate power into human hands, a clear departure from the Shariah-inspired society that Qutb sought to implement, but the Communist society would also deprive Muslims of their basic human need to worship and to live in a spiritual environment. Jihad against this rule, which the Kabul Islamists would soon attempt to implement, was clearly acceptable under Qutb's blueprint. The Kabul Islamists, now led by Rabbani, were acquiring weapons and attempting to infiltrate the Afghan army, but ultimately failed to accomplish anything other than to anger Daoud, who launched a wave of crackdowns on subversive Islamic activity in 1974. Following Daoud's crackdowns on the Islamists, many fled across the border into Pakistan, a country that needed them as much as they needed Pakistan,[152] and the call for Jihad quickly began to spread into the highlands.

In the weeks leading up to Daoud's coup in July of 1973, Jalaluddin Haqqani's life seemed to be on the upswing. He had recently graduated from one of Pakistan's premier madrassas and had been invited back to the Haqqaniyyah School as an instructor. The communists in Afghanistan were worrisome, but Jalaluddin, as an increasingly prominent figure in the Pashtun Deobandi movement, was steadily building up a network of *talibs*

---

[151] Quṭb, Sayyid, and Badrul S. Hasan 52-53
[152] Coll, Steve 114

[students] with whom he hoped to be able to use to liberate Afghanistan with from the rising communist spectre by 1975.[153] He was in the early stages of founding his own madrassah in Paktika, and he had recently campaigned for Jamia Haqqaniyya's headmaster in a successful bid for Pakistan's parliament in the 1970 elections.[154] While he was preparing for a Jihad, Haqqani did not expect the need to come so soon.

Haqqani himself claims that he declared Jihad the moment that he heard about the Daoud coup, despite the fact that Daoud had supported his tribe in the timber disputes of the late 1950s and early 1960s. While there is no evidence that he actually took up arms against the Daoud government until 1975, Haqqani worked to extend his network of contacts to the exiled Kabul Islamists operating out of Peshawar, Pakistan. Gulbuddin Hekmatyar, a fellow highland Pashtun and the most radical of the Kabul Communists, was of particular intrigue to Haqqani, who sent his right hand men to meet with Hekmatyar shortly after Daoud's coup.[155]

Daoud's coup could not have come at a worse time for Pakistan. On December 7, 1970, Pakistan had held its first general elections. With thirty-five competing political parties, it had seemed unlikely that such an election could have resulted in regional civilian governments challenging the military.[156] The military had attempted to cast the elections, in a manner similar to the ongoing struggles in Kabul, as a race between Islam and socialism. Casting the race in such an ideological light would have avoided turning the election into the ethnic battle that Islamabad had such strong reasons to fear, and allowing the Pakistani people to squabble over the nuances of Islamic rule would put the military in a much stronger position than an

---

[153] Brown, Vahid, and Don Rassler 40-42
[154] Brown, Vahid, and Don Rassler 42
[155] Ibid 42-46
[156] Haqqani, Husain 141-142

election based on ethnic nationalism and united attempts at secession could. Such an effort ultimately failed, and the election proved to be the greatest threat to Pakistan's unity, or even to its existence, since Pakistan's conception in 1947.

In Bengali East Pakistan, the Awami League Party won a full seventy-two percent of the vote, winning 167 out of the 169 assembly seats from East Pakistan. In West Pakistan, Zulfikar Ali Bhutto's Pakistan People's Party (PPP) dominated the Punjab and Sindh provinces, while the Pashtuns and Baluchs lent their votes to the Pashtun nationalist National Awami Party and the Deobandi Jamiat-i-Islami Party that Haqqani had been stumping for.[157] The election results sent a clear and immediate message to Pakistan's military establishment—ethnic divisions remained the most divisive force in Pakistani politics, more so than ideological differences. This message would come in even clearer when Mujib Rahman, leader of the Awami League, demanded either autonomy or independence for East Pakistan.[158]

The situation in East Pakistan was resolved through open war. The Pakistani Army, convinced that it had the support of either the United States or the People's Republic of China, intervened with military force against Bengali demonstrators, leading to a military intervention from India. After a short war, Pakistanis tuned in on December 16 to find that Pakistan's forces in East Pakistan had surrendered. With over 90,000 Pakistanis being held by India as prisoners of war, the loss against India, and the imminent loss of East Pakistan, General Yahya's tenure as President of Pakistan was doomed. He was removed by his own military and replaced with Zulfikar Bhutto, the Sindh leader of the PPP. Mujib returned to East Pakistan to become the Prime Minister of the newly established country of Bangladesh.[159]

---

[157] Ibid 143-144
[158] Ibid 146

For Pakistan's military establishment, there were a number of lessons to be learned from this humiliating series of incidents. Pakistan was more divided by its ethnic schisms than by anything else, and Islam, the one uniting factor in Pakistan, was either not strong enough or had not been utilized fully enough to hold the country together. Ideological struggles, such as the struggle between Islam and communism, had not yet captivated the country to the extent that would be needed to in order to distract from the ethnic conflicts. When given the chance, Pakistan's ethnic minorities had jumped at the opportunity to secede from Pakistan, and the military had been unable to prevent such a move. India, the ever present nightmare for Pakistan, was willing to use its military to intervene in Pakistan's internal affairs, and there was nothing that Pakistan could do to prevent India's stronger military from manipulating Pakistan's ethnic divisions to dismantle Pakistan. Perhaps more important than any other lesson though, was that all of these actors and forces could come together to fracture Pakistan to the core, and yet Pakistan's supposed allies in Washington or Beijing would do nothing to stop them. If Pakistan wanted to hold itself together, it would need to act unilaterally and aggressively to defend itself from the forces moving to pull it apart.

With East Pakistan lost, thousands of Pakistani soldiers in Indian custody, India preparing to test a nuclear bomb, and the re-emergence of a known Pashtun nationalist across the border in Afghanistan, the world could not have looked worse from Islamabad. Daoud, having risen to power on the backs of the Parcham communists, had managed to complete the encirclement of Pakistan. A hostile and Soviet-oriented India to the east, a Pashtun nationalist

---

[159] Ibid 152-178

ruler with known ties to Moscow to the northwest, and the desertion of The United States and China, Pakistan's supposed great power allies, meant that Pakistan's very survival would require a miracle.

Daoud, seeking to consolidate his own power, would provide Pakistan with such a miracle. Attempting to secure his own tenuous position as the leader of an Afghan "Republic," Daoud began to surround himself with military officers and to crackdown on those who stood in his way. Communists and Islamists alike were arrested by the hundreds as Daoud turned against ideological rivals, leading many communists to quietly organize for their future after the Islamists fled across the border to Peshawar.

Among the ranks of the thousands of Islamists who fled over the border and into Pakistan were Hekmatyar, Massoud, and Rabbanni, who sought to continue their Jihad from Peshawar. The ISI, which would provide weapons, training, and funding to as many as 5,000 exiled Afghan Islamists over the next two years,[160] began to enlist the mujihadeen leadership that would, for the most part, serve as the vanguard of Pakistan's Afghanistan strategy until the rise of the Taliban in 1994. Pakistani General Naseerullah Babur, running the covert campaign against Kabul, sent Massoud over the border in 1975, hoping that his ISI money and Tajik connections in Afghanistan's Panjshir valley would put enough pressure on Daoud to either weaken him enough to stifle the Pashtunistan issue, or lead to his demise altogether.[161]

These early attempts at overthrowing the Daoud government failed, and perhaps only managed to agitate Daoud, who, for a time, went full steam ahead on support for Pashtun separatists. While Pakistan was using political Islam to bring together a movement that it

---

[160] Brown, Vahid, and Don Rassler 43-44
[161] Coll, Steve 114-116

hoped would act in the interests of the Pakistani government, Daoud took the opposite approach, forgoing ideology to draw on tribal and national identities as a way to put power into the hands of "his people." Confident that Pashtun nationalism and tribal loyalties were stronger than political Islam, Daoud spent the next few years arming, aiding, and coordinating with both Pashtun and Baloch nationalists inside of Pakistan while simultaneously using friendly tribal authorities to continue the crackdown on Islamists.[162] The strategy that Daoud was pursuing was fairly clear—he was attempting to stomp out his enemies by reviving his friendships with his old allies, the highland tribes that he had supported while Prime Minister in the late 1950s and early 1960s, while simultaneously prying open Pakistan's ethnic divisions. Unfortunately for Daoud though, this was not a fight that Pakistan was willing to lose, and a series of economic aid packages worth over a billion dollars from friendly Muslim countries, including Iran and Saudi Arabia, helped Pakistan continue to finance its paramilitary activity against Afghanistan.[163] Pakistan and its ISI would use the money, military experience, Islamic nationalist ideology, and the tribal connections that it had built over the past three decades to undermine Daoud.

Pakistan's strategy in Afghanistan at this point was the same as it had been fifteen years earlier—it was ultimately a strategy that revolved around getting Baloch and Pashtun tribesmen to favor their identity as Islamists over their tribal or ethnic identities. Pakistani media played on the notion that Daoud was an affront to Islam in the hopes that Afghan tribesmen would see his Pashtun nationalism as a Trojan horse for communism, and promoted radical leaders like the Deobandi Haqqani in the hopes that a more potent variety

---

[162] Brown, Vahid, and Don Rassler 42-45
[163] Haqqani, Husain 204-205

of political Islam could stave off ethnic conflict. Such a campaign may not have worked universally, but it worked on enough tribesmen to begin to pressure Kabul.

In August of 1975, while Massoud was still attempting to infiltrate the Panjshir Valley, Hekmatyar, Haqqani, and the ISI were working together to attempt to 'liberate' Paktika from local leaders who were aligned with Daoud. Convinced by Pakistani propaganda that these local warlords were communists, Haqqani attempted to follow Pakistan's line by using Islam as a rallying cry to unify the local highland Pashtuns, potential allies of the Haqqanis, against the government. This strategy payed off when, after intense debate, the tribal elders in Urgun chose to side with Haqqani against the government, but even tribal support would not prevent the inexperienced and poorly trained mujihadeen from being overrun by government forces. The local support proved to be just enough to allow the mujihadeen to escape to fight another day, but the end result was a severe loss of morale among Haqqani's men.[164] The failure to liberate Paktika was just one failure among many mujihadeen failures in 1975, and served to split the mujihadeen into a number of different rival factions, some of which would find so much animosity with each other that they would eventually end up fighting between themselves every step of the way. Despite these failures though, the ISI had managed to pull the tribal authorities away from Kabul in the ongoing tug of war between political Islam and ethnic nationalism.

After the mujihadeen failures of 1975, the border between Afghanistan and Pakistan quieted considerably as both the Pashtunistan and Jihadi issues were put on hold. Shah Reza's Iran, which had become a major financier of Daoud's government, was worried about

---

[164] Brown, Vahid, and Don Rassler 46-49

the situation in Pakistan's Balochistan and, fearing its own Balochi minority, leaned on Daoud to cut his support to nationalist causes. This, combined with Soviet maneuvers intended to warm relationships with Pakistan, forced Daoud to back down from the Pashtunistan issue and warm relationships with the Bhutto government. Daoud ended up visiting Pakistan twice, and even made attempts to work with Bhutto to tone down the separatism and border violence issues.[165] Daoud was limited by these external influences until his murder by scorned communists from the Khalqi faction in 1978.

The repeated defeats of the mujihadeen quieted the Jihadi movement until 1977, when Pakistani internal politics would again shift the direction of Pakistan's Afghanistan policy. The rising wave of political Islam was causing vast internal schisms within Pakistan, whose Islamists increasingly saw Bhutto as an anti-Islamic leader. Another divisive wave of parliamentary elections in 1976 had again threatened to split the country, and Bhutto proved himself to be ineffective at holding back the Islamic tide. As the country moved toward another massive crisis, General Zia ul-Haq, the Army Chief of Staff, sought to ride, rather than push back against, the Islamic wave, and on July 5, 1977, Bhutto was imprisoned and Zia took control of Pakistan.[166]

In the two years left until the Soviet Invasion of Afghanistan, Zia turned the spigot of aid to the mujihadeen back on, and the ISI was given more resources and backing for the mujihadeen than ever before. The mujihadeen activity that Zia was directing would only accelerate after Daoud was murdered by Taraki, who was then murdered by Amin.[167] Zia was

---

[165] Bradsher, Henry S 62-66
[166] Haqqani, Husain 219-224
[167] Brown, Vahid, and Don Rassler 53-56

primarily directing aid to Hekmatyar's Hezb-i-Islam Gulbuddin (HIG), Sayyaf's Ittiad Party, and to Haqqani and Yunis Khalis' Hezb-i-Islam Khalis (HIK). Zia's Zakat Ordinance, one of many campaigns to funnel money into Pakistan's border madrassahs like Jamia Haqqaniyya, combined with the Haqqani's control over pivotal border smuggling routes, ensured that the Deobandi highlanders would continuously receive significant shares of arms shipments and aid money.[168] With Saudi Arabia also donating money by the millions toward Islamic causes in Pakistan,[169] the madrassas quickly eclipsed the waning role of traditional state schools, as parents seeking literacy for their children found the madrassas to be the superior educational experience.[170] It remains unclear exactly how many students these madrassahs would receive over the coming years, but by the time that the Soviets invaded in 1979, Haqqani was dipping into a potent network of Deobandi students and cultivating one of Afghanistan's most formidable militias. By 1977, the heightened resistance and the continued infighting among Afghanistan's communists had already laid the groundwork for the Soviet invasion of 1979. The death of Daoud meant the temporary abatement of the conflict between political Islam and ethnic nationalism, but the battle between Islam and communism was taking on a life of its own.

---

[168] Ibid
[169] Haqqani, Husain 205
[170] Lamb, Christina 97-98

6. A Gift Handed on a Golden Platter

Abdullah Azzam arrived in Afghanistan after a lifetime of ideological struggle. Born in the West Bank village of Seelet al-Hartiyeh, a town near the Syrian border in 1941,[171] Azzam had spent much of his youth organizing against the Israeli occupation of Palestine that had dominated the political landscape of his childhood. In 1962 Azzam crossed the Syrian border to attend Damascus University. While studying the works of Islamic scholars including those of his future role model, Ibn Taymiyyah, Azzam became an early supporter of the Palestinian Liberation Organization (PLO) before graduating with a B.A. in Shariah 1966.[172][173] Following his graduation, Azzam returned home to find a resistance movement very different from the type that he believed could prevail over the Israelis—the Shariah-trained college graduate found that the PLO had been overrun by communists, nationalists, and secularists, and had failed to amount to the Islamic Jihadist movement that had been prescribed by Ibn Taymiyyah.[174] Still though, Azzam, who grew surrounded by and hearing stories of Palestinian refugees, believed that the Israeli occupation of Palestine would only be a temporary nuisance until the day that, victorious over the combined armies of virtually the entire Arab world, Israeli tanks rolled through his village unopposed in June of 1967.[175] The supposed resistance, the supposed strength of Arab nationalism, and the supposed outrage of the Islamic world had failed to stop the billion-strong Ummah from being defeated by six million Jews. Such an event was pivotal to developing a world view in which only an Ummah united by strength in

---

[171] McGregor, Andrew
[172] Azzam, Abdullah. Join the Caravan 1
[173] Azzam, Abullah. Defense of the Muslim Lands 3
[174] Ibid 25
[175] McGregor, Andrew

Islam and strength in Jihad could defeat the foreign invaders.

Even with a resistance movement co-opted by apostates and an Arab world too weak to resist Israel, Azzam knew that he needed to keep fighting. Unable to bear the humiliation of living under the Israeli occupation, Azzam uprooted himself and crossed the border into Jordan, where he spent three years cooperating with the PLO in its effort to resist the Israeli occupation until once again, the governments of the Muslim world failed him. In September of 1970, following a spate of attacks and provocations aimed at King Hussein of Jordan, the Jordanian military cracked down on the Palestinians, killing and expelling thousands of resistance fighters and refugees. Azzam, unable to continue the Jihad against Israel, fled to Cairo to attend al Azhar University, spending three years earning a Ph.D. in the Principles of Islamic Law and mingling with influential members of the Muslim Brotherhood, including the family of the deceased Sayyid Qutb.[176] Living in Egypt in 1973, Azzam had a front row seat to the early promise and eventual loss of the Arab forces in the October Yom Kippur War which, for many in the Muslim world, was the last real chance for the Arab governments to defeat the Israelis. A number of Islamic extremists, including but not limited to the Egyptian Jihadist and future al-Qaeda leader Ayman al-Zawahiri, would later cite the failure of the Arabs in the 1973 war as the final blow to the concept of Israeli vulnerability to the armies of the Arab States.[177]

After the repeated failures to expel the Jews from Palestine, Azzam turned against the Arab governments. Egyptian Jihadists such as Zawahiri had responded to the 1973 failures with a new wave of violence against the Egyptian government and supporters of Arab

---

[176] Azzam, Abullah. Defense of the Muslim Lands 3-4
[177] Al-Zawahari, Ayman, and Laura Mansfield 191-200

nationalism.[178] Azzam, now a prominent member in Muslim Brotherhood circles, provided ideological support to the insurgents throughout the conflict before being expelled by the Egyptian Government, once again a refugee. Azzam, who had now been expelled from his home in the West Bank, his refuge in Jordan, and now his seminary in Egypt, found a temporary home in Jeddah, Saudi Arabia. The House of Saud, a Wahhabi-based government with deep sympathies for exiled Islamists, found Azzam a teaching job at King Abdul Aziz University, where he went on to teach the theories of Qutb, Taymiyyah, and his own emerging beliefs about Islam and Jihad to impressionable Saudi teenagers before he left the campus to attend to the conflict in Pakistan and Afghanistan.[179] Among these teenagers was a wealthy son of a Saudi construction titan, the future holder of the number one spot on the FBI's most wanted terrorists list, and the target of one of the world's largest and most expansive manhunts in history.

Osama bin Laden, one of twenty-five sons of the extraordinarily wealthy and powerful bin Laden family, was a rather ordinary man living an extraordinary life. A product of his surroundings, bin Laden, born in 1957, grew up in an environment that deeply shaped the worldview that, using his vast construction wealth, Osama would inscribe into history.

Future biographers of bin Laden would attribute his radicalism to his days at the al-Thager Model High School, where Osama had been selected by a Syrian soccer teacher who hosted after-school lessons in jihadism. This unnamed soccer teacher, exiled from Syria for radical views and taken in by Saudi Arabia in the same manner as Azzam, selected a young Osama to take part in these radicalization sessions, from which he would emerge as a

---

[178] Ibid 53-39
[179] Baer, Robert 127

"committed schoolyard Islamic activist."[180]

While it is likely that these lessons contributed to his radicalization, the reality is that the young Osama's environment in Saudi society had, since his birth, prepared him for the Jihad that he would take part in through the 1980s. Bin Laden's radicalization was not merely an accident of history, but a natural byproduct of Saudi society.

From birth, bin Laden, like most Saudis, was exposed to Wahhabism, the hardline school of Islam that, like the Deobandi school, is rooted in a literalist interpretation of the Quran. Founded in the 18th century by Muhammad ibn Abd al-Wahhab, the spread of the Wahhabi school has been one of the greatest forces for life in the political jihad movement.

In 1716, at the age of 12, Al-Wahhab embarked on a pilgrimage that took him across the Arab world. It was in Basra, a city in modern day Iraq, where Al-Wahhab noticed that something was very wrong with the way that Islam was being interpreted. Muslims were worshiping holy tombs and shrines, including shrines to the Prophet Muhammad. People prayed for saints to intervene in worldly affairs. People worshiped trees, and thought that talisman and amulets had magical properties. The land was filled with imposter magicians and sorcerers claiming to have superhuman powers. Al-Wahhab, shocked by the world around him, vowed to put an end to these blasphemous practices. Like the Deobandis, he began to preach that Islam needed to be purified, and returned to the literal teachings of the Quran and the Sunnah in an attempt to end the blasphemous practices of tomb worship, sorcery, and mysticism.[181]

Al-Wahhab was kicked out of Basra and returned home to Arabia, where he finished

---

[180] Coll, Steve "Letter from Jeddah: Young Osama." 59
[181] Baer, Robert 84

developing his teachings, which soon became a detailed code of how to properly follow a literalistic interpretation of the Quran, leading to oddly literal instructions on "how to sneeze, embrace, shake hands, yawn, kiss, dress and so on. There [is] even a Wahhabi way of reinterpreting physics; strict Wahhabis believe the world is flat."[182]

After being kicked out of Basra, and then again being kicked out of the Arabian town of Al ʿUyaynah, al-Wahhab fled southeast to the town of Dar'iya, where he met Muhammad ibn Sa'ud, great-great-great-great-grandfather of the Muhammad ibn Saud who would go on to found the modern state of Saudi Arabia. The marriage between the Sauds and the Wahhabis continues today, with Wahhabi Islam being the official sect of Saudi Arabia, and Wahhabis use state approved madrassahs and mosques to entrench militant Wahhabi Islam as a fundamental part of Saudi life.[183]

Al-Wahhab fundamentally believed that the enemies of Islam were rooted in polytheism and expressed themselves through the blasphemous idol worship that he had seen in Basra, as well as through other religions such as Judaism. Al-Wahhab spent the rest of his life fighting alongside the Sauds to wage Jihad against non-believers, mysticism and the improper practice of Islam until his death in 1792. Al-Wahhab's words are today taught to children in madrahsas, homes, and mosques in Saudi Arabia and across the Islamic world. A young Osama Bin Laden likely came under the influence of these words well before he attended his high school.

The Wahhabi ideology that engulfed the Arabian Peninsula was destined to dominate bin Laden's worldview from his birth. Mirroring al-Wahhab, Osama's father Mohammad

---

[182] Baer, Robert 85
[183] Baer, Robert 84-90

instilled in a young Osama the perennial hatred of Israel and the Jewish people, as well as the need to fight to reclaim Muslim lands.[184] The elder bin Laden's wealth and networking put bin Laden, while still in high school, into contact with the leaders of the low level Islamic insurgency in Afghanistan, including Rabbani and Sayyaf. The Wahhabi upbringing, the hatred of Israel, and his contacts with the mujihadeen leaders combined to, at a young age, bring bin Laden into contact with the texts of ibn Taymiyyah.[185] Like Abdullah Azzam, the geopolitics of the modern Islamic world had buried a young Osama into the texts of the 13th century father of Jihadi doctrine and, like Azzam, these texts would soon come to play an important part in Osama's worldview.

Like Azzam, bin Laden uprooted himself within weeks of the Soviet invasion, traveling to Pakistan to begin a career in Jihad.[186] On his decision to travel to Afghanistan, bin Laden writes that:

> "This so called 'Great Russian Bear' surprised the world in 1979 by invading Kabul with its military machine, via routes from Tajikistan, Uzbekistan, and Turkmenistan. The situation at the time was one of a clash between Western Capitalism and Soviet Communism. The Soviets succeeded in convincing many of the Islamic and Arab states to accept their corrupt ideology. The race between the two superpowers to achieve world domination is commonly referred to as the 'Cold War.'
>
> Nobody had anticipated that the small state of Afghanistan, with its meager resources, would be able to resist the advances of the Red Army...The Communist Party had arisen in Afghanistan and began to invite people to clear and manifest disbelief. Some of the scholars and youth tried to respond to this with *Dawah* [proselytizing] activities, but their financial resources were very

---

[184] Scheuer, Michael 37-41
[185] Ibid 41
[186] Ibid 64-65

limited and they were unable to repel this threat. Therefore, Allah blessed the mujihadeen leadership with the ability to raise the banner of Jihad."[187]

In a lengthy introduction to one of Azzam's many publications, bin Laden described how the geopolitical situation in Afghanistan, one in which it appeared that the communists were prepared to waltz through a Muslim land, had instead created the conditions for the Islamists to rally around a jihad and fend off the Soviets.

Following the call for foreign fighters from Jalaluddin Haqqani, trickles of foreign fighters were making their way into Afghanistan to join the ranks of the mujihadeen,[188] creating the beginnings of a network of Arabs that joined the predominantly Pashtun and Tajik resistance movement. These Arabs quickly went to work, with some, such as Azzam, joining the fight on the frontlines, while others, such as bin Laden, worked their networks to raise funds, distribute food, build hospitals, and do other humanitarian work to aid both the mujihadeen and the growing Pashtun refugee population in Pakistan.[189] Among these foreign part-fighter part-humanitarian workers was the Egyptian Jihadist Ayman an al-Zawahiri.

Zawahiri, a doctor by trade, had arrived in Peshawar in 1980 as part of a Muslim Brotherhood coordinated relief effort for the Afghan mujihadeen.[190] Zawahiri had spent the last two decades attempting to foment the type of Jihad in Egypt that was now occurring in Afghanistan, but by his own admission, his attempts in Egypt had consistently been unsuccessful because of his failure to build a secure rear base. The four months that Zawahiri spent on his first visit to Afghanistan were "a gift handed on a golden platter."[191] The terrain in

---

[187] Azzam, Abdullah. The Lofty Mountain 79-82
[188] Brown, Vahid, and Don Rassler 61-62
[189] Scheuer, Michael 65-66
[190] Al-Zawahari, Ayman, and Laura Mansfield 26-28
[191] Ibid 26

Egypt, clusters of urban environments offering refuge from two flat and inhospitable deserts, had made finding such a base impossible. Afghanistan, with its large rural population and untamable mountainous hinterland, proved to be a much more suitable environment for Jihad.[192]

Zawahiri's choice to aid the Afghan Jihad was, like many of the Kabul Islamists now fighting against the Soviets and the Karmal government, partially a result of Sayyid Qutb. In his own words, Zawahiri claims that:

> "Qutb affirmed that the issue of unification in Islam is important and that the battle between Islam and its enemies is primarily an ideological one over the issue of unification. It is also a battle over to whom authority and power should belong—to God's course and shari'ah, to man-made laws and material principles, or to those who claim to be intermediaries between the Creator and mankind.
>
> This affirmation greatly helped the Islamic movement to know and define its enemies. It also helped it to realize that the internal enemy was not less dangerous than the external enemy was and that the internal enemy was a tool used by the external enemy and a screen behind which it hid to launch its war on Islam"[193]

Unifying the Ummah—the Pashtuns, the Arabs, and the Tajiks, the Wahhabis, the Deobandis, and the Muslim Brothers—under one conception of Jihad, would be the only way for the Islamic world to unite over the secularists, the crusaders, the Americans, the Jews, and the other forces seeking to carve up the Muslim world and impose secular governments. Thus, when the opportunity to work with a purely Islamic resistance arose, a resistance free from the influences of nationalism, western liberalism, or communism,[194] such an opportunity

---

[192] Ibid 26-40
[193] Ibid 47
[194] Ibid 33-34

appeared to Zawahiri to be a divine act of destiny.[195] By the end of his second tour of the region, Zawahiri had come to pinpoint the Afghan Jihad as the focal point of the Islamic world. It was in Afghanistan, unlike in Palestine, Egypt, or other battlegrounds, where the Ummah had the most potential to unite under one untainted ideology. Like Azzam and Qutb, Zawahiri believed this to be the key ingredient in the recipe for success. Zawahiri left Egypt in 1981 to preside over the assassination of Egyptian President Anwar al-Sadat, and after a three year stint in Egyptian jail, returned to Afghanistan in 1986.[196]

By Zawahiri's 1986 return, Azzam and bin Laden had become quite busy. In 1981, Jalaluddin Haqqani, funded by the American, Saudi, and Chinese money that was beginning to flow through the ISI, had set up a training camp in Loya Paktika that accepted the non-Afghan fighters and was preparing to build a second camp in Khost, just miles from the border with Pakistan.[197] Among these trainees was Abdullah Azzam who, while fighting alongside the Haqqanis in 1982, wrote a series of journal articles intended for Arabic-speaking youths based upon miracles that he had 'witnessed' in Afghanistan, articles that were compiled into a book that was released in 1983.[198] Filled with extravagant claims of mujihadeen surviving every infliction from bullets (which magically bounced off of their bodies)[199] and Soviet tanks that drove over mujihadeen without crushing them,[200] to name some of the less fantastical examples (others include cows or bags of raisins warning of impending Soviet advances), Azzam's book, *Signs of the Merciful,* is also littered with quotes

---

[195] Ibid 29
[196] Ibid 35
[197] Brown, Vahid, and Don Rassler 66-68
[198] Hegghammer, Thomas 41
[199] Azzam, Abdullah, and A. B. Al-Mehri 46
[200] Ibid 38

both attributed to and about Haqqani. Azzam, who heaps praise on Haqqani, was clearly being influenced by the prominent Deobandi scholar, and following the sweeping success of *Signs of the Merciful*,[201] Azzam was prepared to release his seminal and groundbreaking work, *The Defense of Muslim Lands*.

Inspired by Haqqani, ibn Taymiyyah and Sayyid Qutb, *The Defense of Muslim Lands* is today considered to be *the* revolutionary doctrine on Jihad (copies of the book are still being distributed among Jihadists around the world, including ISIS fighters in Iraq and Syria). In this book, Azzam declares that when the kufr (non-Muslims or infidels) enter a Muslim land, "expelling the kufr from our land is Fard Ayn (a compulsory duty upon all). It is the most important of the compulsory duties."[202] Previous doctrines had written that it is the duty of those who live in the invaded areas to expel the invaders, but Azzam takes it a step further, writing that:

> "If the Kufr enter a Muslim Land: In all Islamic ages, Jihad under this condition becomes Fard Ayn upon the Muslims of the land which the Kufr have attacked and upon the Muslims close by, where the children will march forth without the permission of the parents, the wife without the permission of her husband, and the debtor without the condition of the creditor. And, if the Muslims of this land cannot expel the Kufr because of lack of forces, because they slacken, are indolent, or simply do not act, then the Fard Ayn obligation spreads in the shape of a circle from the nearest to the next nearest. If they too slacken or there is gain a shortage of manpower, then it is upon the people behind them, and on the people behind them, to march forward. This process continues until it becomes Fard Ayn upon the whole world."[203]

What Azzam is envisioning here is the creation of a transnational Jihad, one where

---

[201] Hegghammer, Thomas 41
[202] Azzam, Abullah. Defense of the Muslim Lands 15
[203] Ibid 16

Muslims from across the Islamic world travel the globe to do the job that the ideologically corrupted governments had been unable to do. Azzam goes on to ask that all potential Jihadists temporarily forgo the Palestinian cause and begin with defending Afghanistan because, in agreement with Zawahiri, Azzam believes that the terrain and Islamic spirit of the Afghan cause are naturally better suited for Jihad than anywhere else in the world. Despite the fact that billions of American and Chinese dollars were flowing into the hands of the mujihadeen, Azzam did not believe that the Afghan cause had not been corrupted in the way that the Palestinian cause had.[204] This definition of jihad, one stemming from a lifetime of ideological struggle, remains at the forefront of the jihadi movement.

Azzam's determination to forgo regional struggles in favor of the larger struggle was not without controversy. Many scholars fundamentally disagreed with Azzam's interpretation of Islamic law, and many Jihadist leaders did not wish to forgo their local causes for the mountains of the Hindu Kush. The controversy though, may have only served to increase the proliferation of his fatwa, which soon became a hit throughout the Arab world. In the second half of 1984, shortly after the release of Azzam's influential fatwa, the flow of non-Afghan fighters into Afghanistan began to accelerate.[205]

As the new wave of Arab fighters was beginning to arrive in Afghanistan, bin Laden and Azzam again coalesced around each other as they both grappled with the question of what to do with the influx of Arabs arriving in Peshawar.[206] These fighters needed to be fed, clothed, sheltered, trained, and brought onto the battlefield, and the various Afghan mujihadeen

---

[204] Ibid 17
[205] Hegghammer, Thomas 41-42
[206] Scheuer, Michael 67-74

factions, some of which frowned on the fundamentalism of the Arab volunteers altogether, lacked the capabilities to fill such a void. Seeing this need, the duo combined bin Laden's fortune with Azzam's influence to found Makhtab al-Khadamat (MAK), also known as the Afghan Services Bureau. With offices all over the world, including Europe and the United States, bin Laden and Azzam were creating a transnational network capable of bringing in cash and mujihadeen from across the globe while releasing and distributing propaganda through magazines, cassettes, and videotapes. Azzam and bin Laden were beginning to usurp local clerics by using MAK's media arm to distribute sermons worldwide, and naturally, these sermons carried Azzam's message of global Jihad.[207]

MAK's longest lasting legacy was its role in organizing and distributing Arab fighters into the Jihad. After four years of fighting and networking, bin Laden and Azzam were naturally both partial to their favorite commanders, and as a result, a majority of MAK fighters wound with the highland Pashtuns Haqqani and Hekmatyar, while others were sent to fight with Sayyaf, the favored commander among Wahhabi donors.[208] [209] These three factions, the factions most prone to fundamentalist Islam, were a natural fit for bin Laden, but after two years of distributing MAK fighters, Azzam began to have other ideas about where to allocate his troops.

By 1986, Ahmed Shah Massoud, the Lion of Panjshir, had earned a reputation as one of the most effective battlefield commanders on the Afghan battlefield. After a series of failed attempts to raise an army following his exile in 1973, Massoud again returned to Panjshir in

---

[207] Ibid
[208] Ibid 74
[209] Coll, Steve 85-89

1978 with a handful of rifles and a declaration of Jihad against the Taraki government. Within five years, he had trained one of the most effective and disciplined armies in Afghanistan and, using tactics from the playbooks of Mao Zedong and Che Guevara, Massoud had taken such a toll on the Soviet Army that he had managed to negotiate a temporary truce with senior Soviet commanders as high up as Yuri Andropov. [210] The truce was temporary, but negotiations with the Soviets, combined with the fact that he was both an ethnic Tajik and a relatively moderate Muslim, served to discredit him in the eyes of fundamentalist commanders and the Pakistanis, who felt that supporting a non-Pashtun and non-fundamentalist commander would only serve to push the Pashtuns back towards the Pashtunistan issue. The ISI began to support other mujihadeen commanders, particularly Hekmatyar, as they launched devastating attacks against Massoud and his Tajik population. Under fire from the Soviets and other Afghan commanders, Massoud rose to stardom using little more than the weapons and supplies captured from ambushed Soviet convoys, leaving him dramatically underpowered compared to the Pakistan or Saudi backed factions led by Hekmatyar, Haqqani, and Sayyaf.[211]

Azzam was a fundamentalist by any definition of the word, but the myriad of writing that Azzam produced shows that he was also interested in winning the war, and he saw Massoud as a capable commander.[212] Unlike the Deobandis or Wahhabis, Azzam was not raised on the Quranic literalist ideology that others had been indoctrinated by. As the man responsible for the hordes of young men traveling to fight in the Jihad and a man who now spent much of his time surrounded by these 'Afghan Arabs,' Azzam naturally believed that the

---

[210] Ibid 119-122
[211] Ibid 109-126
[212] Scheuer, Michael 74-75

Arabs were significant forces in the war, even as many Afghan commanders rejected the use of these fighters.[213] Regardless though, Azzam felt that bringing the MAK soldiers to the Tajik north to fight under Massoud could cut Soviet supply lines and turn the tides of the war in favor of the mujihadeen.

Osama though, was beginning to have different plans altogether. The foreign weapons that were piling up in Afghanistan had naturally forced the ISI to develop a number of different networks, safehouses, and storage units for both weapons and fighters that they were smuggling into Afghanistan. One of the largest of these storehouses was residing in the Zhawara Valley within Khost province, just four kilometers from the border with Pakistan. This base, within Haqqani territory, routed up to a full third of ISI-smuggled weapons into Afghanistan, and included a mosque, a pro-mujihadeen Deobandi radio station, and by 1986, had become one of the few large training facilities that accepted Arab fighters. Bin Laden, who was increasingly becoming convinced that MAK should build its own transnational Islamic army rather than merely be responsible for distributing fighters, jumped on the opportunity and sent large numbers of MAK recruits to train while simultaneously using his family's construction equipment to build and fortify the compound.[214]

The Soviets, aware of the enormous weapon cache and training facilities at Zhawara, launched a full scale assault on the complex in March of 1986. The Haqqanis and their ISI handlers fought valiantly against communist Afghan forces backed by Soviet helicopter gunships, but by April 19, heavy fighting had pushed the Haqqanis back and allowed the Soviets to push through Zhawara's defenses. Haqqani put out a call for aid, and on April 20, a

---

[213] Coll, Steve 154
[214] Brown, Vahid, and Don Rassler 66-71

contingent of Arab fighters, led by bin Laden and Azzam, arrived to meet with Jalaluddin to coordinate a counterattack. For the first time, MAK recruits fought together as organized units, and within hours, they had pushed the Soviets and their Afghan allies away from the Zhawara compound.[215]

Bin Laden was rewarded for his support with three caves that were to be used exclusively by MAK for training and storage within the Zhawara compound but, emboldened by his first major battlefield victory, bin Laden was dreaming of a more ambitious plan. He began using his family's construction equipment to build a new facility near Jaji, slightly north of Zhawara. Over the objections of Azzam, who felt that the base was a misallocation of resources and a fundamental split from the role of MAK, the base, also known as both The Lion's Den and as **al-Qa'ida** al-'askariyya, soon emerged to rival bin Laden's other base at Zhawara as the core training facility for Arab fighters. Both facilities handily eclipsed the MAK facilities in Pakistan.[216]

Azzam still believed that the core mission of the Arabs was to integrate with the Afghan mujihadeen, merely offering them assistance in their own struggle. Bin Laden though, perhaps a more geopolitical thinker, saw Afghanistan as the center of a global struggle, and his army as the liberators of the entire Muslim world, not just as a support structure for the Afghan mujihadeen. Bin Laden did not merely want his men to assist Afghans in the liberation of Afghanistan, but instead wanted to build a platform with which he could mobilize to defend the Islamic cause around the globe. The return of Zawahiri, who also saw Afghanistan as a potential base to target Egypt from, only served to reinforce bin Laden's

---

[215] Ibid 70-74
[216] Ibid 74-77

view.

Over the next three years, bin Laden would use the tale of his valor at Zhawara and subsequent battles near Jaji to become a media celebrity, frequently moving between Jaji and Peshawar to take interviews, produce videos, and spread his face and message around the world. He turned the influx of fighters into a regular army which, no longer distributed amongst mujihadeen units, fought along and even lead Pashtuns units at the 1989 Battle of Jalalabad and beyond. In 1988, Azzam temporarily reconciled with bin Laden to join him and Zawahiri in the christening of al-Qaeda, an organization that would work to take bin Laden's armed forces, his vast financial networks, and their combined ideological and propaganda sway to field recruits from across the Muslim world and prepare them for Jihad. It is unclear how closely Azzam intended to coordinate MAK with al-Qaeda, but following Azzam's assassination in 1989, bin Laden took over MAK and effectively merged the two, inheriting the personnel and the ideological clout that Azzam had left behind.[217]

Al-Qaeda was born out of an attempt to bridge the gaps in the Muslim world, bringing fighters from North Africa, Central Asia, South Asia, the Caucus, and elsewhere in the Islamic world under one flag. Bin Laden sought to use his army and financial resources to support Islamic causes against communists in Yemen, against Saddam Hussein following Iraq's 1991 invasion of Kuwait, against Christian forces in the Balkans, and in a myriad of other conflicts that he envisioned al Qaeda support for. As a transnational movement, al-Qaeda, even with its various leadership struggles, had a plethora of enemies to unite against. After the Soviet pullout from Afghanistan though, the struggle between Islam and Communism quickly turned

---

[217] Scheuer, Michael 82-93

into a struggle between different Islamist factions.

With the Soviets leaving and the Afghan communists relatively inept, the establishment of an Islamic State in Afghanistan seemed imminent. Pakistan continued to funnel tens of millions of dollars in aid to the Haqqanis and to Hekmatyar as they turned toward Kabul. Even before the Soviets had left though, Hekmatyar had turned his long running dispute with Massoud into a full scale civil war that continued beyond the collapse of the Afghan Communist Government in 1992. In 1994, facing an utterly dysfunctional Afghan society that had rescinded to different fiefdoms and constant civil war, the ISI switched its allegiance from Hekmatyar to the Taliban, a newly emerged Deobandi movement composed primarily of highland Pashtuns.[218] Most of the Taliban's leadership had studied in Jamia Haqqaniyya, and the new movement made natural allies with the Haqqanis. By 1996 the two Pashtun Deobandi factions, backed by the ISI, had cooperated to defeat Hekmatyar and to put Massoud and his Turkic allies on the defensive.

Bin Laden and Zawahiri used the victory over the Soviets to proclaim a new era in the Islamic world, one in which Islam prevailed over the world's second largest superpower and, at least within the Islamic world, it was no longer to be a struggle between Soviet-backed communists and Western-backed autocrats, but between a global Jihadist movement and those who sought to restrict or oppress Islam. Pipe dreams of reuniting old empires, tearing down the boundaries of states, and overthrowing secular governments were born out of Qutb and Azzam's writings on Jihad and were inspired by the mujihadeen victory in Afghanistan. Often backed by returning Arab fighters or even bin Laden himself, fighters returning from

---

[218] Brown, Vahid, and Don Rassler 101-105

the war soon sparked or played a role in waves of religious violence in former Soviet republics, China's Xinjiang Province,[219] Algeria, Yemen, Egypt, and beyond.

Pakistan remains a country struggling with an existential lack of national unity. Pakistan is home to several divided ethnic groups, almost all of which have expressed separatist ambitions. In order to keep the ambitions of these different ethnic forces at bay, the Pakistani government has done everything in its power, including supporting radical mosques, madrassahs, and militias that promote building one's political identity around Islam rather than ethnicity or tribe. Islamabad also maintains a deep fear over India, and attempts to use support for Islamic militants in Kashmir to undermine Indian authority over the disputed region. Such militants, backed by the ISI, have often been based in Afghanistan, sharing training spaces and cooperating with al-Qaeda and the Haqqanis.[220] Pakistan's "Islam over Tribe" strategy and its obsession with Kashmir has lead Pakistan to support both the Haqqani Network and the Taliban until the present day, even as the state itself comes under attack from elements with ties to these groups. Such support will likely be deemed necessary until the day that the state itself is dissolved among revisionist Islamic militants.

One of the largest effects of the war though, was perhaps its role in uniting different variations of Sunni Islam around one struggle. A Wahabbi from Saudi Arabia, Muslim-Brotherhood oriented men from Egypt, a Palestinian, and Pashtun Deobandis from Afghanistan's tribal region come from vastly different worlds, yet, fighting together, they made some progress on bridging the gaps between their different units.

Such unity though, is not total, and Afghanistan has not left the state of civil war that it

---

[219] Millward, James. 24-40
[220] Brown, Vahid, and Don Rassler. 237-239

entered in 1973. Different mujihadeen leaders, out of personal power struggles, cultural and ideological differences, along with ethnic ad tribal divisions, spent much of the war clashing amongst themselves rather than fighting the Soviets, and continued to clash among themselves after the Soviet pullout. Even MAK and al-Qaeda, organizations created specifically to bridge differences in the Islamic world, struggled early and often with leadership and ideological disputes. Today, different Al-Qaeda organizations find themselves fighting each other in Syria, where personal power struggles between al-Qaeda leaders have played out in the form of bloody clashes between the groups known as the *Islamic State in Iraq and al-Sham* and *Jabhat al-Nusra*. Despite the disunity between rebel factions in Syria today though, the legacy of the Soviet-Afghan war is affirmed as foreign fighters once again rush to leave their homes to fight the Jihad against the Alawite 'kufr'.

As of yet, there does not yet appear to be an equivalent to Azzam or bin Laden in terms of financial, logistical, or ideological capabilities, and Zawahiri appears to be commanding a much smaller force than bin Laden did at his peak of power. As fronts for Jihad continue to flare up in North Africa, the Levant, Iraq, Central Asia, and the Arabian Peninsula though, the mujihadeen efforts against the Soviets, both organizational and ideological, will continue to have a fundamental influence on the geopolitical situation in the Islamic world for decades to come. Infighting will be the norm for quite some time, but the proliferation of a transnational political identity rooted in a shared perception of Jihad will continue to transform the world for years to come.

Conclusion

Three superpowers entered a war in Afghanistan. After a bloody loss, one left the mountains of the Hindu Kush a crippled mess, and a new force, political Jihadism, moved in to replace the Soviet Union as a major player in Asian geopolitics. The war that helped to accelerate the sudden end of the Cold War had demonstrated the enmity between the People's Republic of China and the Soviet Union while simultaneously highlighting the ongoing struggle between religious unity and national or tribal divisions within the Islamic world. While nothing in such a complex conflict is black and white, twenty years of maneuvering by the Soviets and the Chinese, the long-running dispute between Pashtun nationalists in Afghanistan and Pakistani statists, and Islam's repeated failures to prevent schisms within Pakistan compellingly trace a path to war.

Communism, a force once touted as an unstoppable wave of the future, had failed to unite the two great socialist powers, the Soviet Union and the People's Republic of China. The schism between the two, based on diverging national interests and geopolitical realities, led to the redistribution of Asian's power structure as the Soviets and Chinese were forced to strategize against each other. Multiple disputes within Asia, including Sino-Soviet border skirmishes, the 1962 Sino-Indian War and the 1979 Sino-Vietnamese War, showed how serious the Chinese and the Soviets were in their struggles against each other and pushed both states to intervene against the other in Afghanistan.

The Soviet-Afghan War was merely one phase of a much longer struggle between a potential political unification under Islam and the divisive nature of tribal and ethnic conflicts in South Asia. The Pakistanis have repeatedly shown that promoting radical Islam was not merely a temporary measure taken in response to the Soviet invasion, but is instead a long running strategy designed to defend Pakistan from the political realities of the divisive ethnic and tribal forces in the region. Support for radical Islamists, which has now evolved into support for militias based around the Deobandi School of Islam, is likely to continue until there is a fundamental alteration in the direction of either Afghan or Pakistani politics, and will remain a danger to global security for the considerable future.

Al-Qaeda, a group that was itself born out of a leadership dispute, was created as an attempt to bridge the ethnic and ideological gaps between Arabs, Pashtuns, Chechens, Turks, and other races, as well as between Wahhabis, Deobandis, Muslim Brothers, and other ideological factions. The group though, has struggled with leadership disputes, and is now divided by an intra-organizational civil war in Syria, arguably the biggest threat to the group's cohesiveness since its foundation. The rifts within political jihadism have yet to be managed.

The breakup of the Soviet Union provided a temporary halt to the great geopolitical contests for Central Asia. Islam though, emerged from the Soviet-Afghan War with renewed vigor as a political ideology with potential to captivate the region. Perhaps, as with communism, political Islam may one day disintegrate under the combined weight of ethnic divisions, ideological disputes, and the failure of Islamic rule to produce viable economies capable of feeding the growing populations in the Muslim world. Until that day comes though, the Pakistani strategy of supporting political Islam as a counterweight to ethnic divisions, as it spreads through the Islamic world, is likely to continue to advance despite the struggles for unity that it faces.

Works Cited

Al-Zawahari, Ayman, and Laura Mansfield. *His Own Words: Translation and Analysis of the Writings of Dr. Ayman Al Zawahiri*. Old Tappan, NJ: TLG Publications, 2006. Print.

Arne Westad, Odd, Chen Jian, Stein Tønnesson, Nguyen Vu Tungand, and James G. Hershberg. *77 Conversations Between Chinese and Foreign Leaders on the Wars in Indochina, 1964-77. Cold War International History Project*. Woodrow Wilson International Center for Scholars, May 1998. Web. 15 Sept. 2013.

Azzam, Abdullah, and A. B. Al-Mehri. *Signs of Allah the Most Merciful in the Jihad of Afghanistan*. Birmingham, UK: Maktabah, n.d. Print.

Azzam, Abdullah. *Join the Caravan*. London: Azzam Publications, 1996. Print.

Azzam, Abullah. *Defense of the Muslim Lands*. N.p.: Brothers in Ribatt, 1984. Print.

Baer, Robert. *Sleeping with the Devil: How Washington Sold Our Soul for Saudi Crude*. New York: Three Rivers, 2004. Print.

Bradsher, Henry S. *Afghanistan and the Soviet Union*. Durham, NC: Duke UP, 1983. Print.

Brown, Vahid, and Don Rassler. *Fountainhead of Jihad: The Haqqani Nexus, 1973-2012*. New York: Oxford UP, 2013. Print.

Carter, Jimmy. "The State of the Union Address Delivered Before a Joint Session of the Congress." *The American Presidency Project*. University of California Santa Barbara, n.d. Web. 24 Nov. 2013.

"China Condemns Soviet Military Invasion of Afghanistan." *Beijing Review* 23.1 (1980): 3-4. Print.

Coll, Steve. *Ghost Wars: The Secret History of the CIA, Afghanistan, and Bin Laden, from* the Soviet Invasion to September 10, 2001. New York: Penguin, 2004. Print.

Coll, Steve. "Letter from Jeddah: Young Osama." *New Yorker* 12 Dec. 2005: 48-61. Print.

Crile, George. *Charlie Wilson's War: The Extraordinary Story of the Largest Covert Operation in History*. New York: Atlantic Monthly, 2003. Print.

Dalrymple, William. *The Return of a King: The Battle for Afghanistan, 1839-42*. New York: Alfred A. Knopf, 2013. Print.

Dikötter, Frank. *Mao's Great Famine: The History of China's Most Devastating Catastrophe, 1958-1962*. New York: Walker, 2010. Print.

Eftimiades, Nicholas. *Chinese Intelligence Operations*. Annapolis, MD: Naval Institute, 1994. Print.

Gates, Robert M. *From the Shadows: The Ultimate Insider's Story of Five Presidents and How They Won the Cold War*. New York, NY: Simon & Schuster, 1996. Print.

Haqqani, Husain. *Magnificent Delusions: Pakistan, the United States, and an Epic History of Misunderstanding*. New York: PublicAffairs, 2013. Print.

Haroon, Sana. "The Rise of Deobandi Islam in the North-West Frontier Province and Its Implications in Colonial India and Pakistan 1914-1996." *Journal of the Royal Asiatic Society* 18.1 (2008): 47-70. *JSTOR*. Web. 14 Mar. 2014.

Hegghammer, Thomas. *Jihad in Saudi Arabia: Violence and Pan-Islamism since 1979*. Cambridge, UK: Cambridge UP, 2010. Print.

"How to Deal with Soviet Hegemonism." *Beijing Review* 22.13 (1979): 23-25. Web.

Ibn Taymiyyah, Taqi Ad-Din Ahmad. *The Religious and Moral Doctrine of Jihaad*. Birmingham, England: Maktabah Al-Ansaar, 2001. Print.

"Interview of Vice-Premier Deng Xiaoping by U.S. TV Commentators." *Beijing Review* 22.7 (1979): 17-20. Print.

Kaplan, Robert D. *Soldiers of God: With the Mujahidin in Afghanistan*. Boston: Houghton Mifflin, 1990. Print.

Kissinger, Henry. *On China*. New York: Penguin, 2011. Print.

Lamb, Christina. *The Sewing Circles of Herat: A Personal Voyage Through Afghanistan*. New York: HarperCollins, 2004. Print.

Mashal, Mujib. "Hekmatyar's Never-ending Afghan War." *Al Jazeera*. Al Jazeera Media Network, 28 Jan. 2012. Web. 24 Nov. 2013.

McGregor, Andrew. ""Jihad and the Rifle Alone": 'Abdullah 'Azzam and the Islamist Revolution." *Journal of Conflict Studies* 23.2 (2006): n. pag. *The Gregg Centre for the Study of War and Society*. University of New Brunswick, Feb. 2006. Web. 18 Mar. 2014.

Millward, James. *Violent Separatism in Xinjiang: A Critical Assessment*. Issue brief. Washington: East-West Center, 2004. Print.

"Moscow's 'Dumb Bell' Strategy." *Beijing Review* 23.8 (1980): 8-9. Print.

Nasr, Vali. *The Shia Revival: How Conflicts Within Islam Will Shape the Future*. New York: Norton, 2006. Print.

Olesen, Asta. *Islam and Politics in Afghanistan*. Richmond, Surrey: Curzon, 1995. Print.

People's Republic of China. Embassy of the People's Republic of China. United States of America. *Joint Communiqué of the People's Republic of China and the United States of America*. N.p.: n.p., 1972. Print.

Quṭb, Sayyid, and Badrul S. Hasan. *Milestones*. Karachi: International Islamic, 1981. Print.

Reagan, Ronald. "Address Before a Joint Session of the Congress on the State of the Union." *The American Presidency Project*. University of California Santa Barbara, n.d. Web. 24 Nov. 2013.

Scheuer, Michael. *Osama Bin Laden*. New York: Oxford UP, 2012. Print.

Snow, Edgar. "A Conversation with Mao Tse-Tung." *LIFE* 30 Apr. 1971: 46-48. Web.

Soviet Union. Central Committee. Politburo. *Account of the Decision of the CC CPSU Decision to Send Troops to Afghanistan*. By Alexander Lyakhovsky. Moscow: n.p., 1995. *National Security Archive*. George Washington University, 13 Oct. 2012. Web. 19 Nov. 2013.

Soviet Union. Central Committee. Politburo. *Meeting of the Politburo of the Central Committee of the Communist Party of the Soviet Union, March 17, 1979*. N.p.: n.p., n.d. Print.

Soviet Union. Komitet Gosudarstvennoy Bezopasnosti. Archive of the President of the Russian Federation. *Personal Memorandum from Yurii Andropov to Leonid Brezhnev*. By Yurii Andropov. N.p.: n.p., 1979. *National Security Archive*. George Washington University, 13 Oct. 2012. Web. 19 Nov. 2013.

Soviet Union. Komitet Gosudarstvennoy Bezopasnosti. *Memorandum on Afghanistan*. By Yuri Anropov, Andrei Gromyko, Dmitry Ustinov, and Boris Ponomarev. N.p.: n.p., 1979. *National Security Archive*. George Washington University, 13 Oct. 2012. Web. 19 Nov. 2013.

Starr, S. Frederick. *Xinjiang: China's Muslim Borderland*. Armonk, NY: M.E. Sharpe, 2004.

Print.

"Three Principles for Solution to Afghan Issue." *Beijing Review* 23.11 (1980): 3. Print.

Tomsen, Peter. *The Wars of Afghanistan: Messianic Terrorism, Tribal Conflicts, and the Failures of Great Powers*. New York: PublicAffairs, 2011. Print.

United States of America. Central Intelligence Agency. *Soviet Options in Afghanistan*. N.p.: n.p., 1979. *National Security Archive*. George Washington University, 13 Oct. 2012. Web. 19 Nov. 2013.

United States of America. Department of State. Embassy Kabul. *Six Weeks after Afghanistan's Revolution*. Kabul: n.p., 1978. Print.

United States of America. Department of State. Embassy of the United States of America in Beijing, China. *Joint Communiqué on the Establishment of Diplomatic Relations between the People's Republic of China and the United States of America*. N.p.: n.p., 1979. Print.

United States of America. The White House. National Security Council. *Reflections on Soviet Intervention in Afghanistan*. By Zbigniew Brzezinski. Washington D.C.: n.p., 1979. Print.

United States of America. White House. National Security Council. *Summary of Conclusions: SCC Meeting on Soviet Moves in Afghanistan*. N.p.: n.p., 1979. *National Security Archive*. George Washington University, 13 Oct. 2012. Web. 23 Nov. 2013.

United States of America. The White House. National Security Council. *U.S. Policy, Programs, and Strategy in Afghanistan*. Intelligence Resource Program, n.d. Web. 21 Nov. 2013.

United States of America. White House. National Security Council. *What Are the Soviets Doing in Afghanistan?* By Thomas Thornton. N.p.: n.p., 1979. Print.

Wawro, Geoffrey. *Quicksand: America's Pursuit of Power in the Middle East*. New York: Penguin, 2010. Print.

Xin, Chanlin. *Beijing Review* 22.24 (1979): 22-24. Web.

Xin, Ping. "Soviet Union Steps Up Southward Drive." *Beijing Review* 22.31 (1979): 23-26. Web.

Yu, Pang. "Aggressors Must Be Punished." *Beijing Review* 23.3 (1980): 9-10. Print.

Yu, Pang. "New Tsarist Challenge." *Beijing Review* 23.2 (1960): 9-12. Print.

Made in the USA
Monee, IL
15 June 2020